SEDONA

50 Memorable Landscapes

Photography

By

Al Lodwick

Any errors of commission or omission are the responsibility of the author and do not reflect on those who offered their opinions on the content.

First Edition 2015

ISBN: 978-1514875841

DEDICATION

To Ann Lodwick, my wife and best friend for nearly thirty-eight years.

ACKNOWLEDGEMENTS

Scott Mies for encouragement and editorial advice.

Rachel Lodwick for the Mieswick, LLC logo.

Victoria Tubbs for the author's photograph.

INTRODUCTION

It is a cliché to say that "words fail" but this is never truer than when trying to describe the area around Sedona, Arizona. At the nearby V-BAR-V Heritage Site there is a crack in a rock with a petroglyph next to it that is thought to be a depiction of a spirit entering the "other world". It is thought that this spirit image was made by someone who lived in the area as far back as 900 years ago. The minimum that you can say about the Sedona region is that people have thought of it as a spiritual place for a long time. Today's adherents of what we call "main line" religions have taken advantage of some beautiful settings to erect their places of worship. The more modern "New Age" religions have drawn many people to the area in recent times. Even if you see the area in "scientific terms' it is difficult to resist feeling a sense of awe at the energy expended by wind, water and tectonic forces to develop these landscapes.

I feel extremely privileged to live so close to this beautiful place that I could get up almost any morning and say to my wife, "Let's go to Sedona for lunch today", and we would.

As unbelievable as it may seem, Photoshop was only used to crop and enhance color. Nothing was added to these pictures that did not appear in the original photographs.

Words fail – the pictures are presented without comment.

Al Lodwick
Prescott, Arizona
July 2015

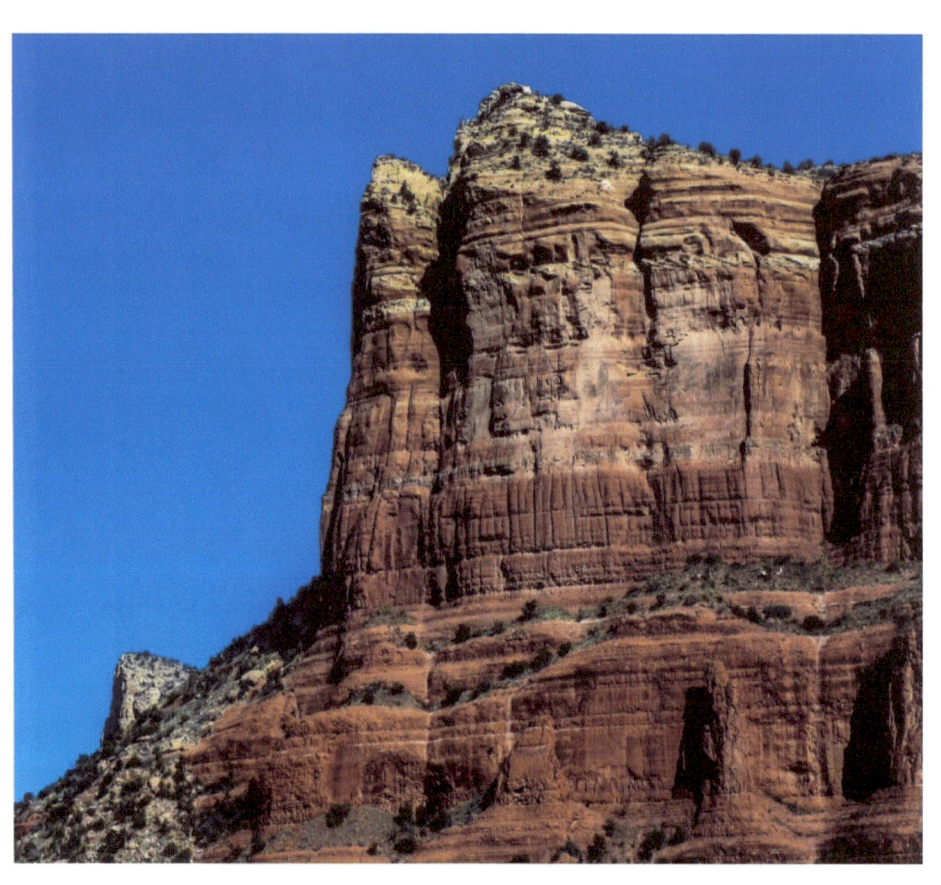

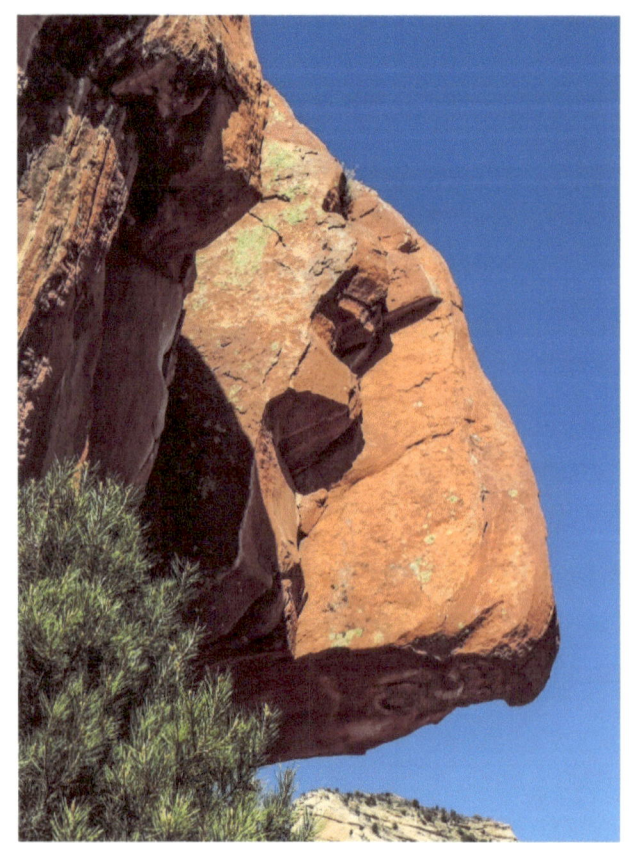

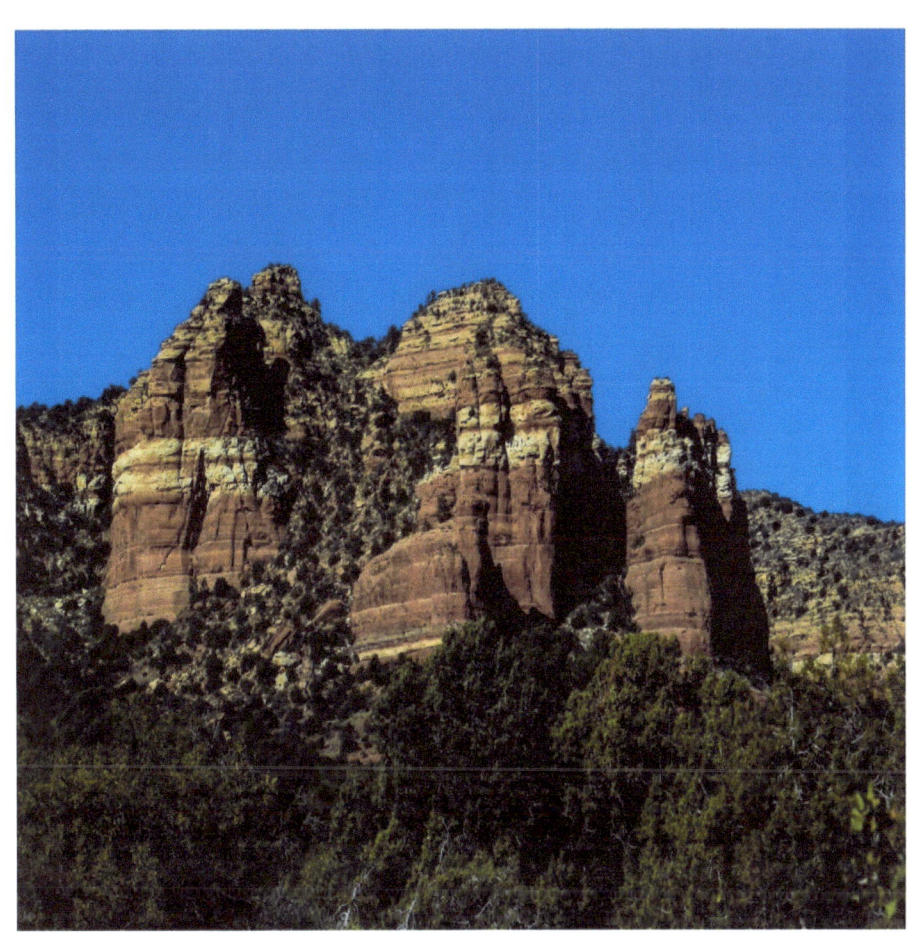

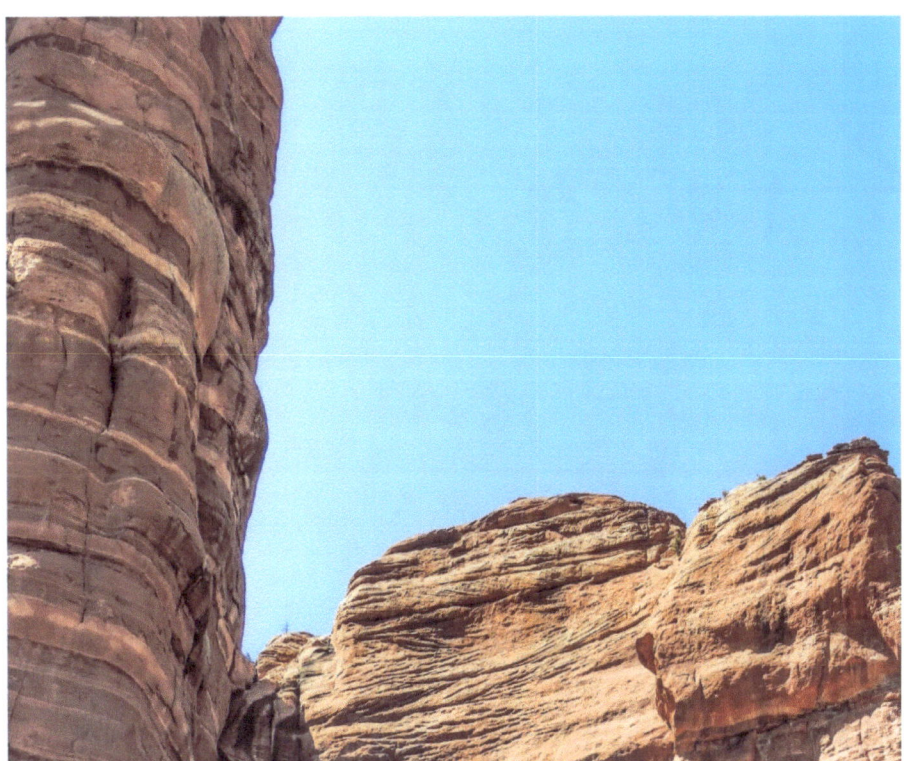

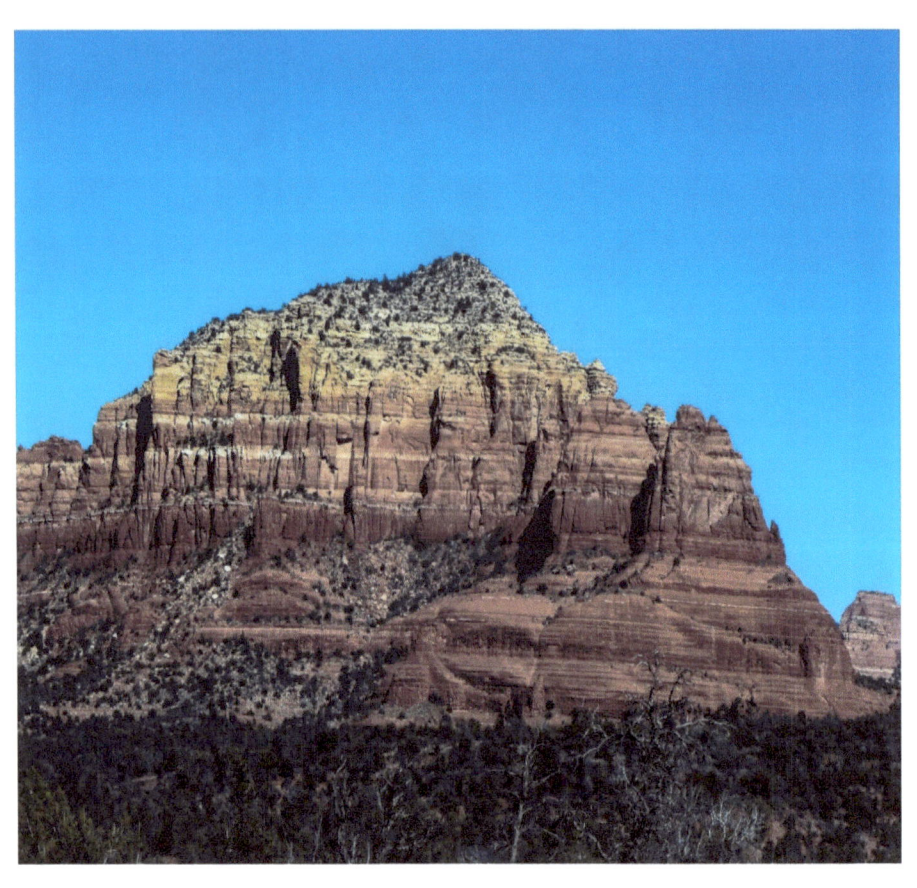

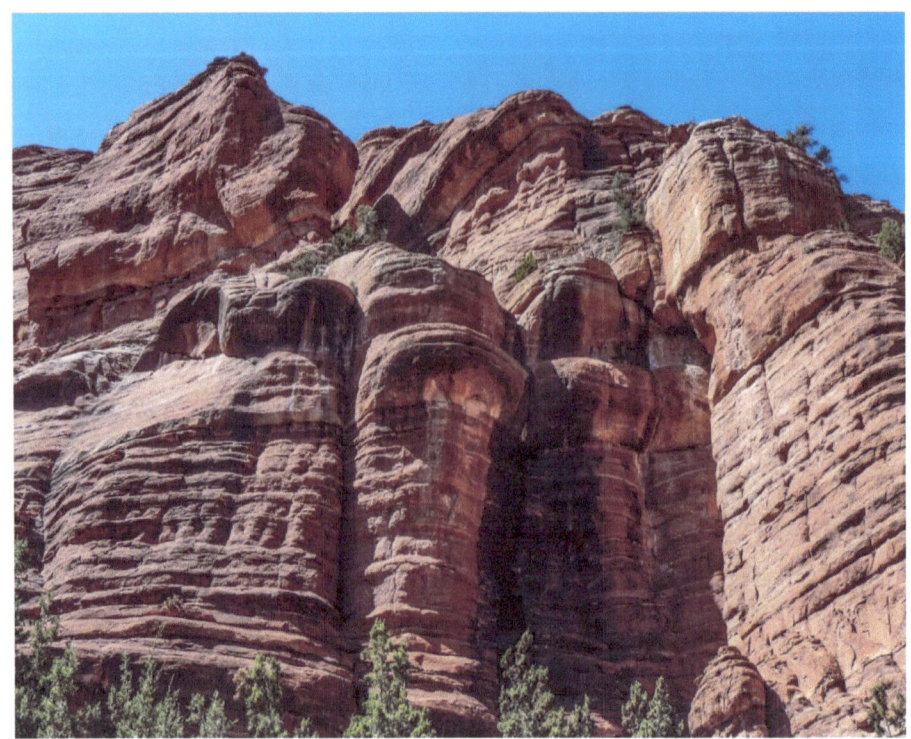

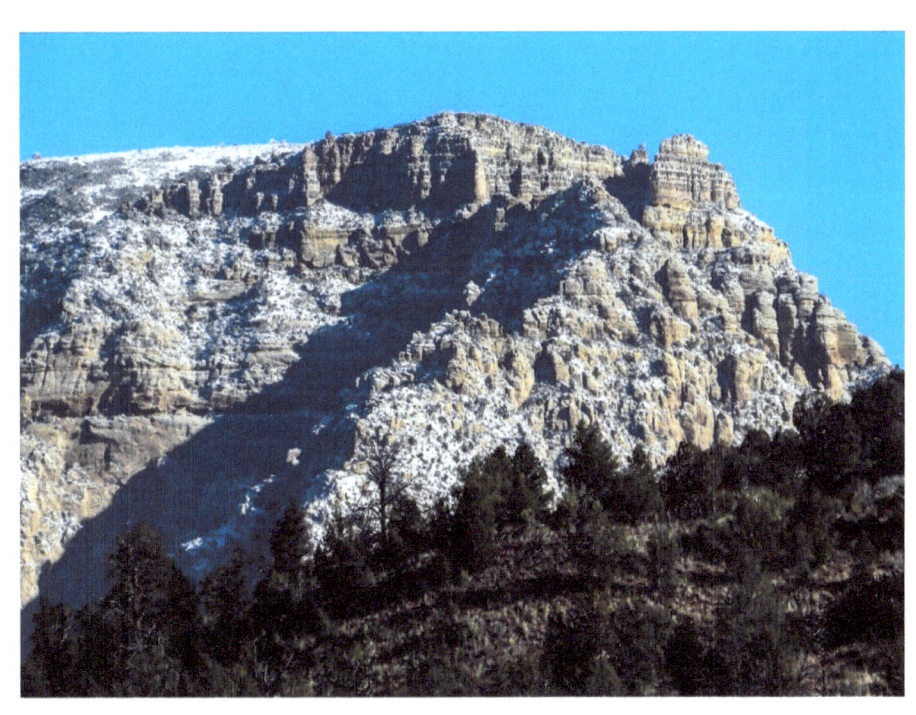

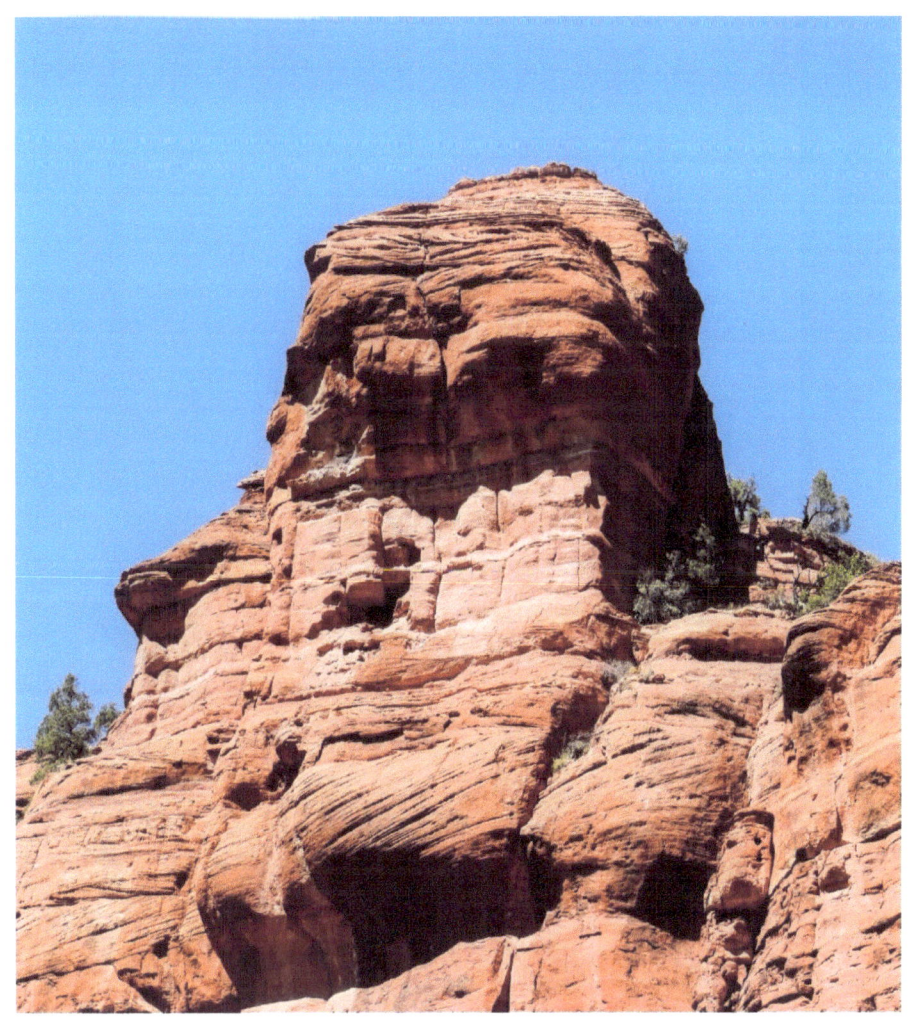

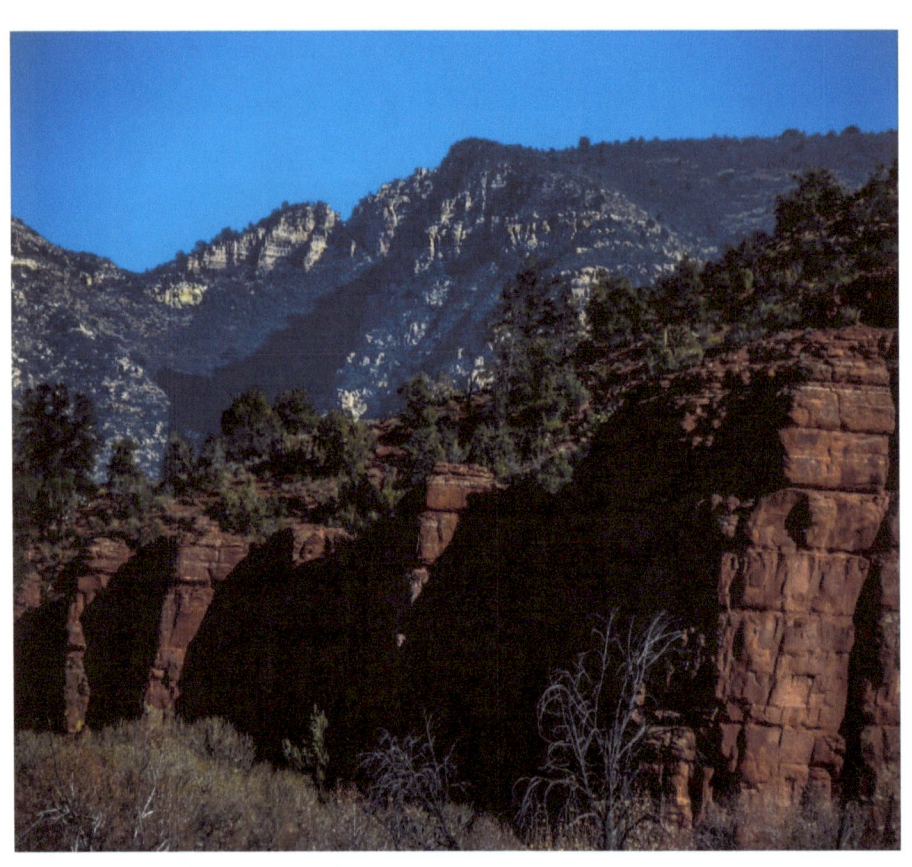

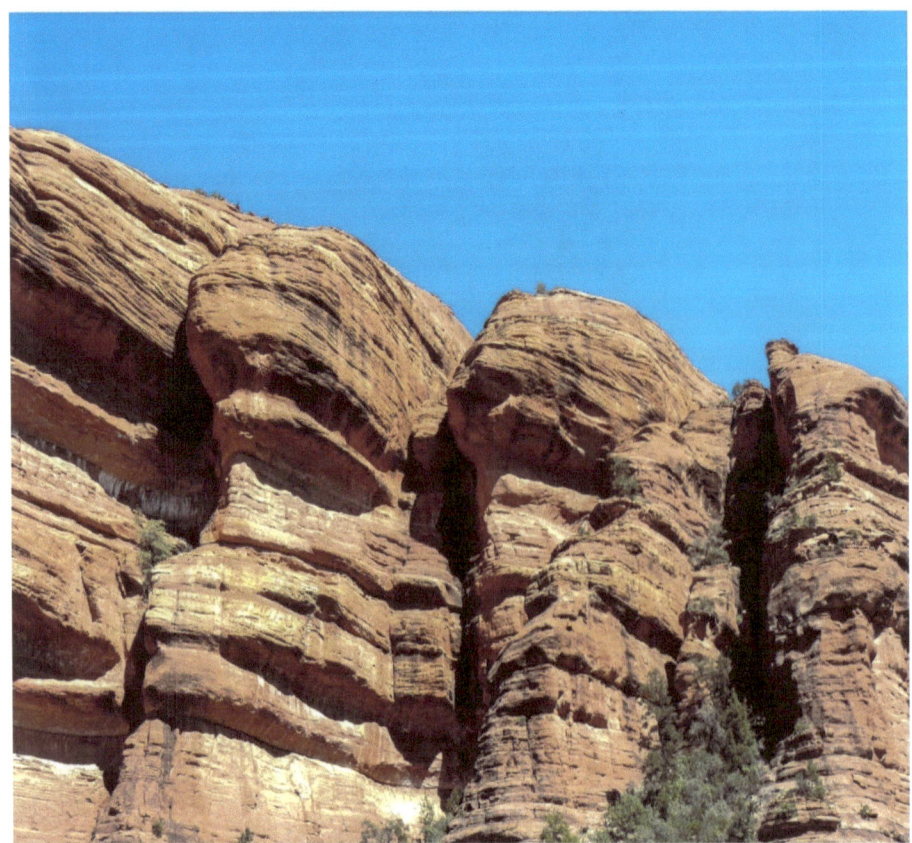

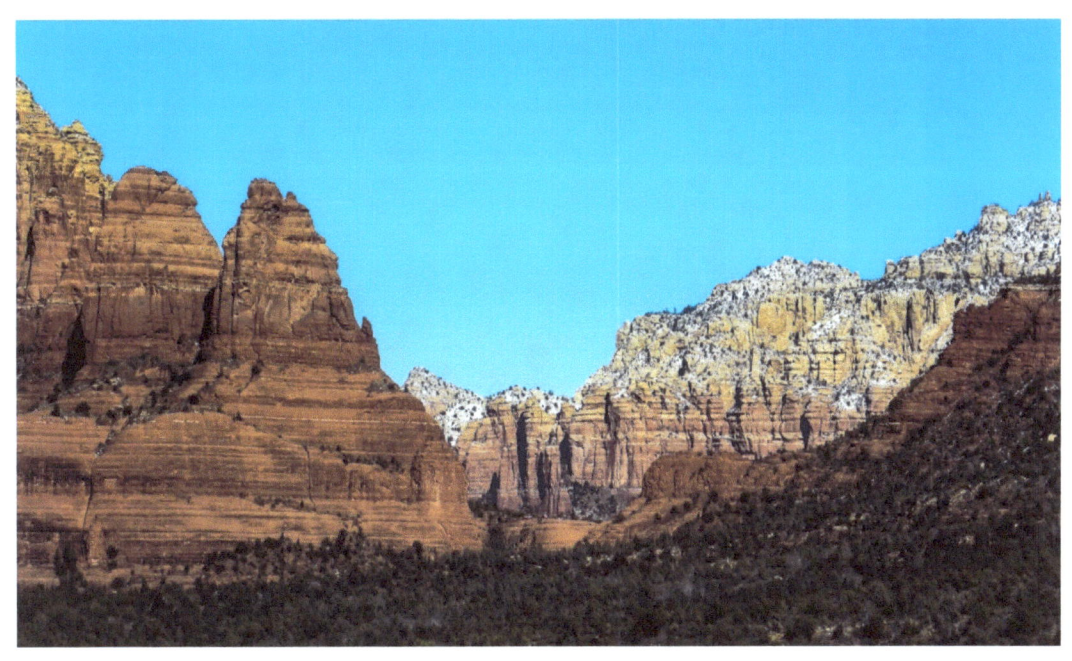

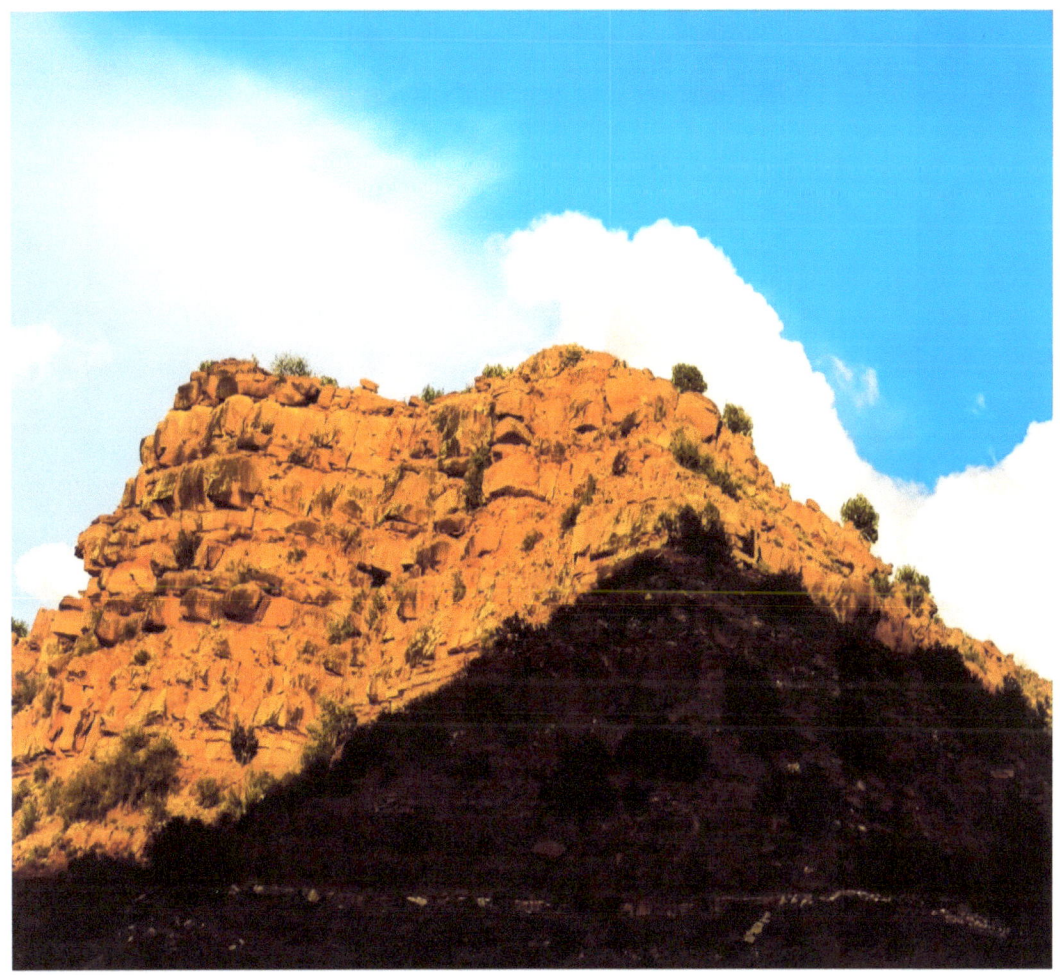

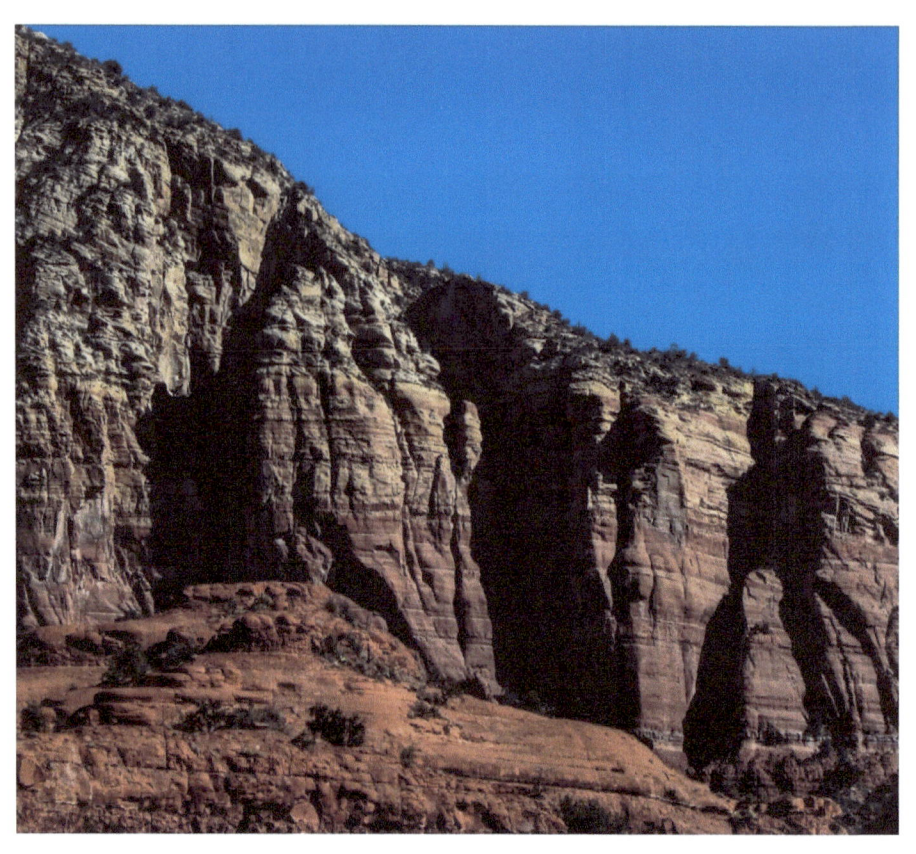

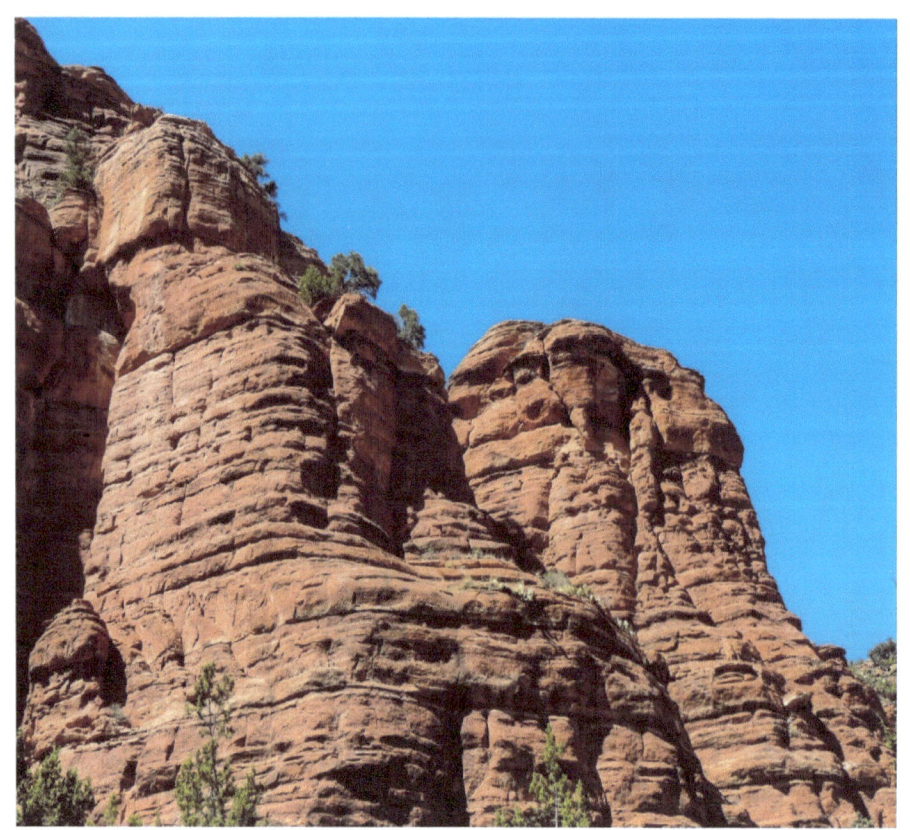

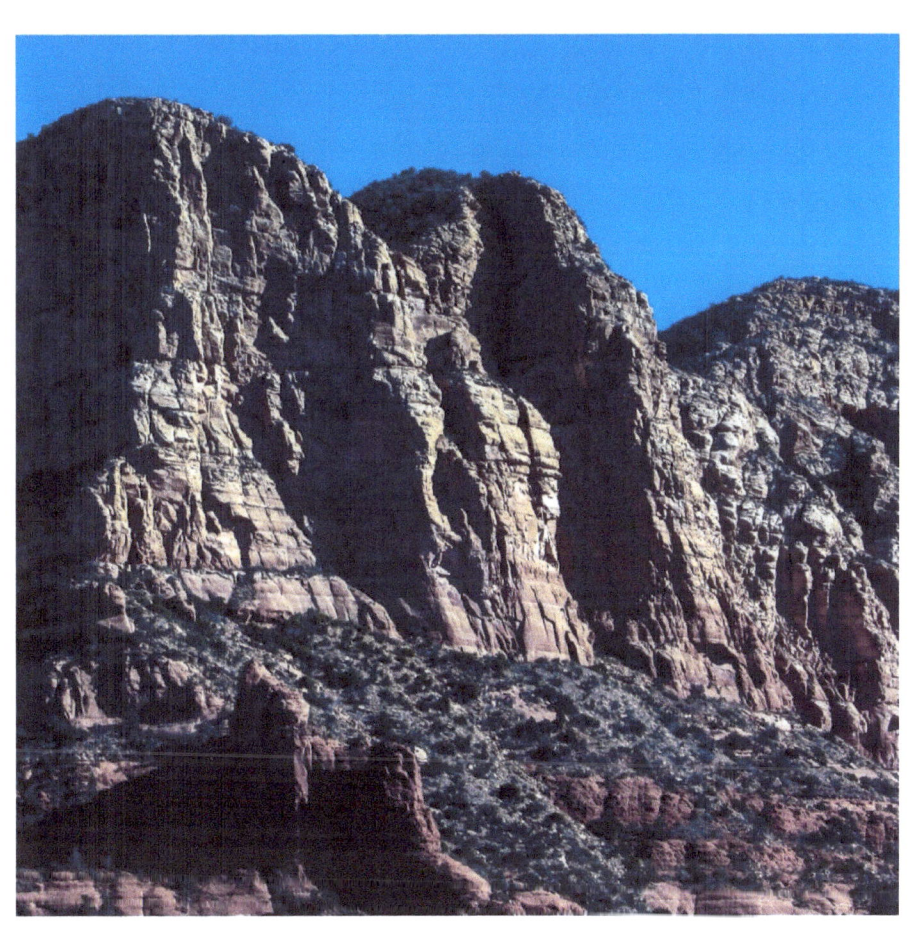

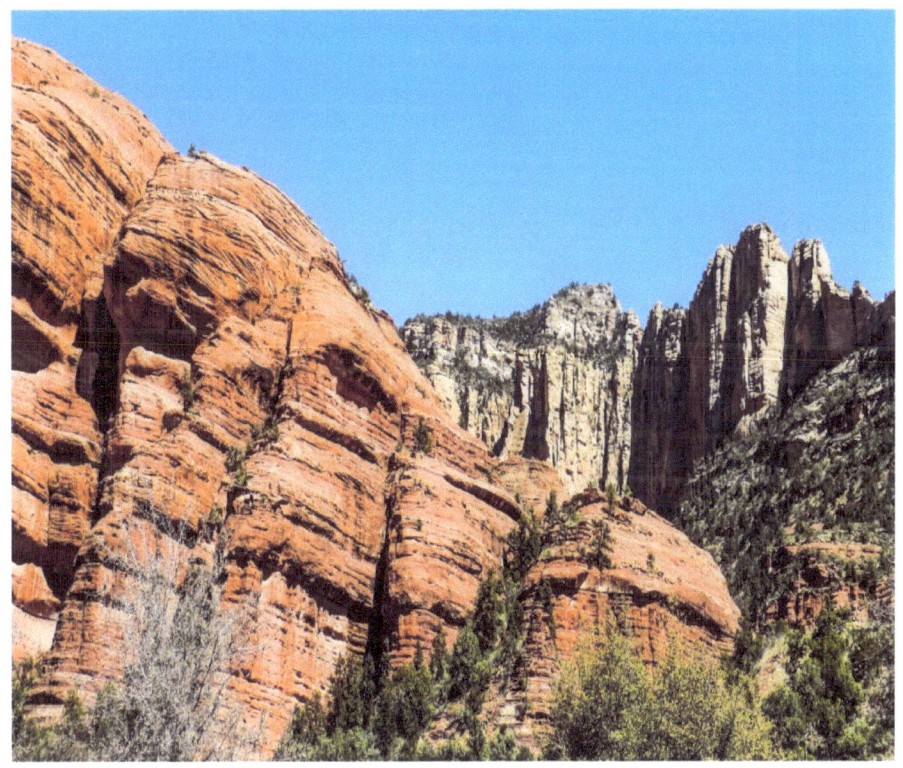

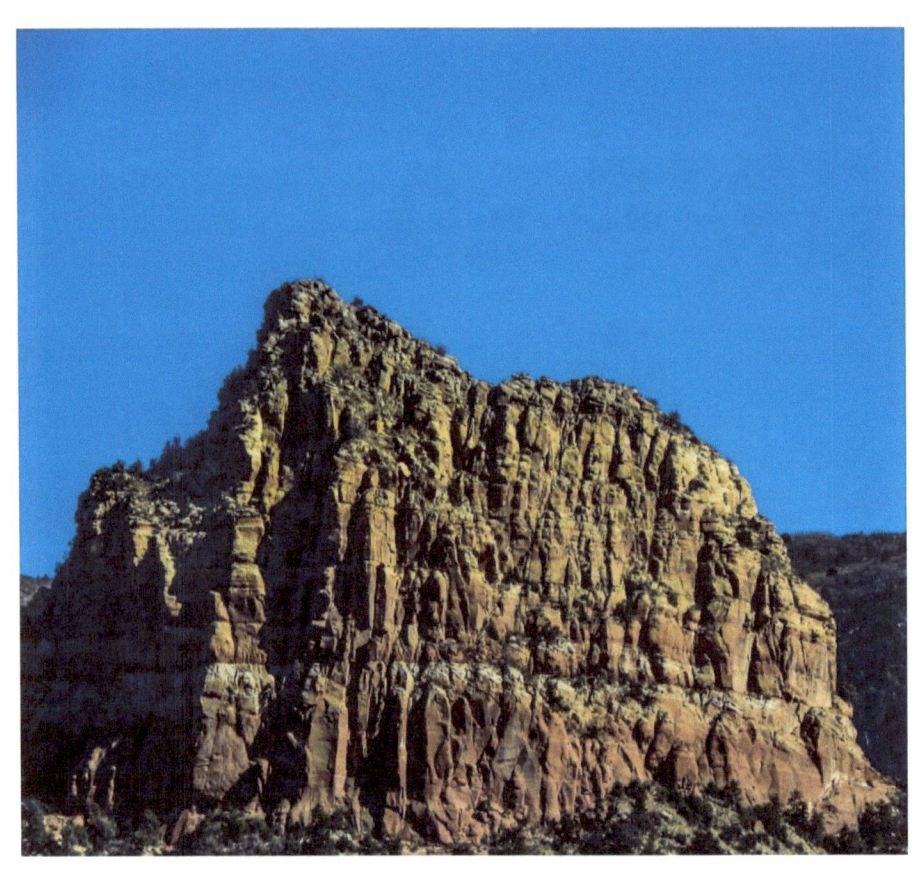

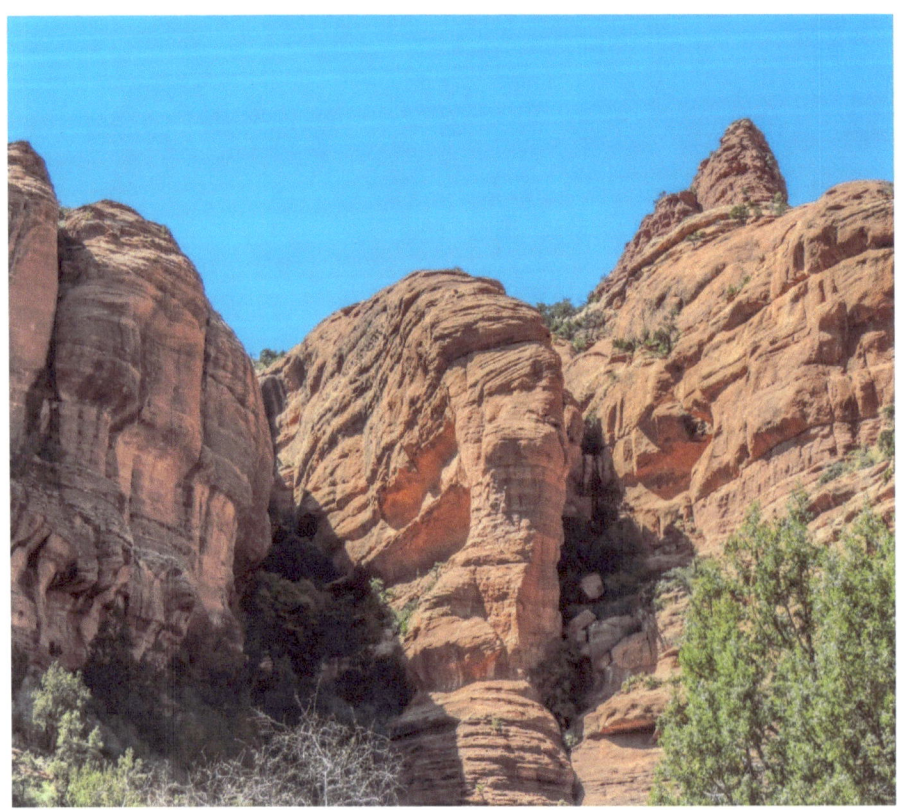

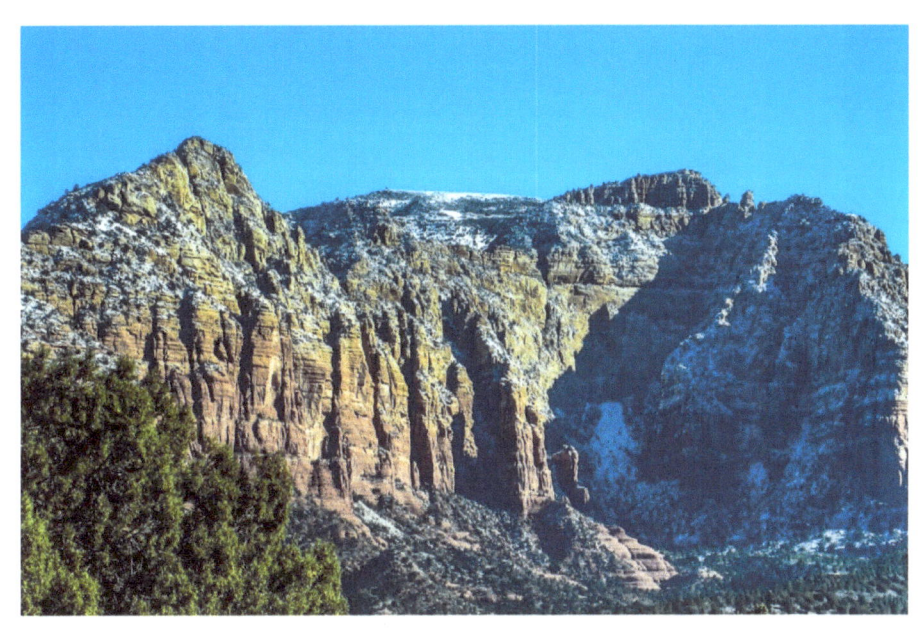

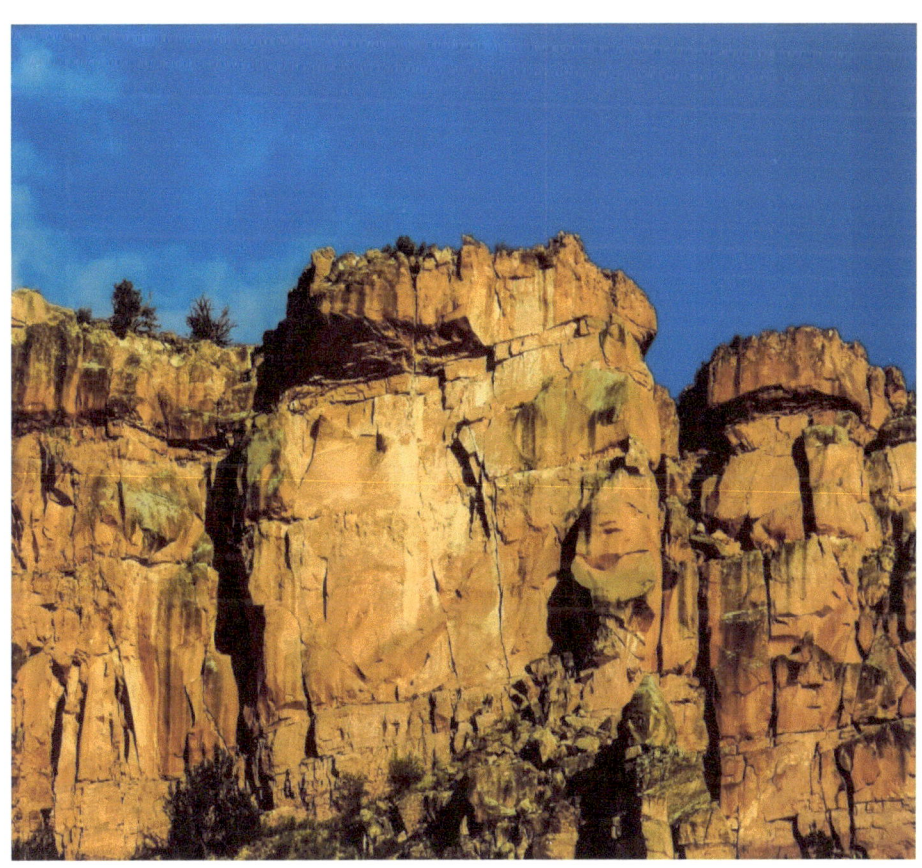

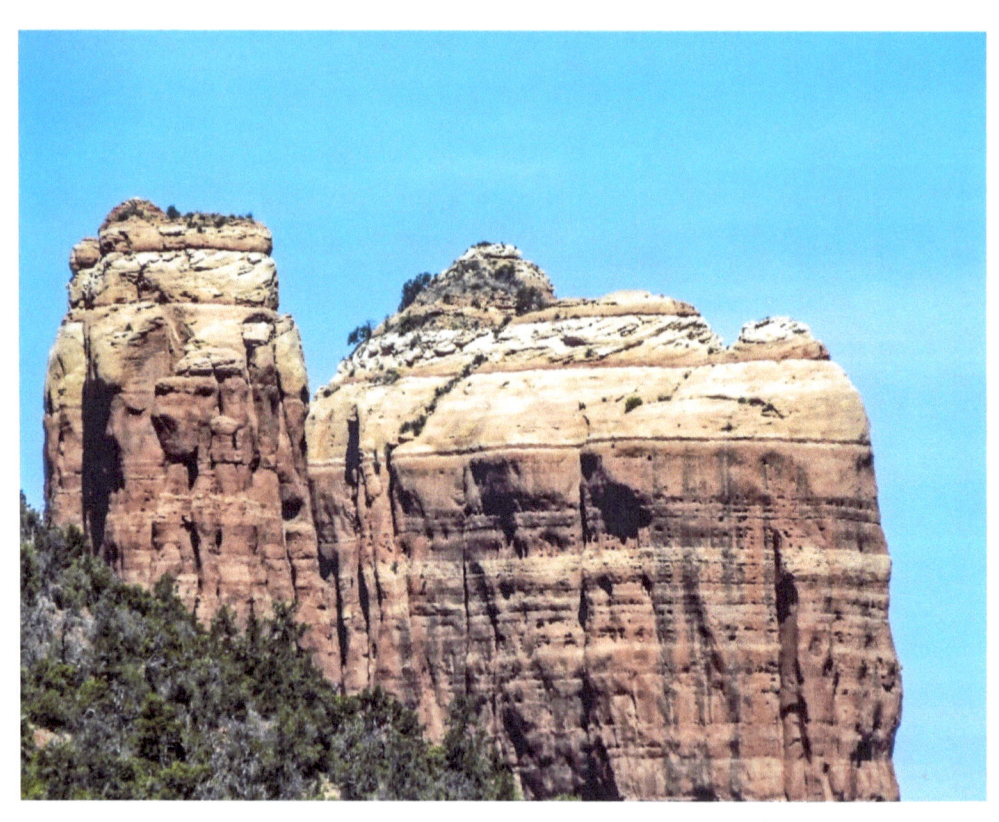

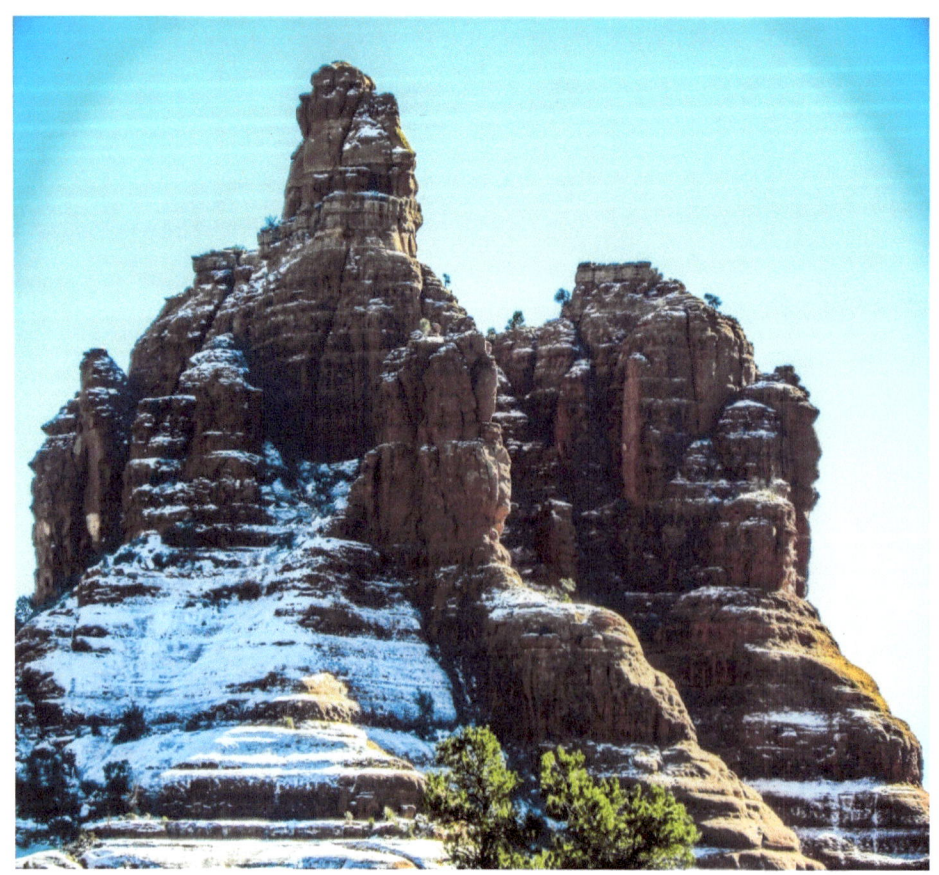

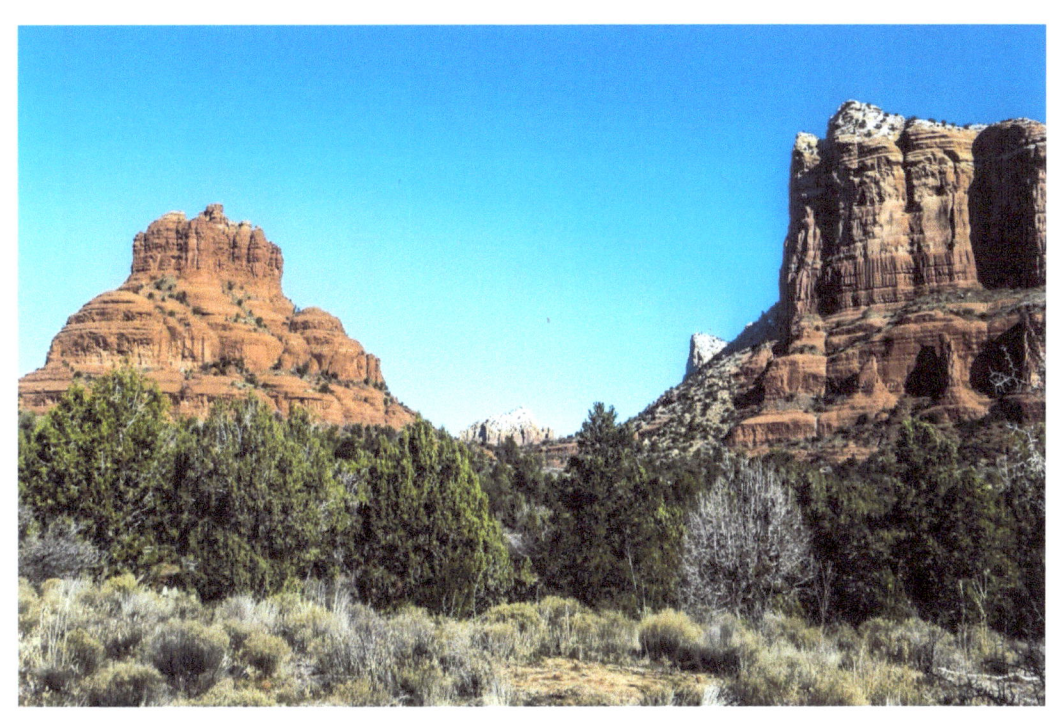

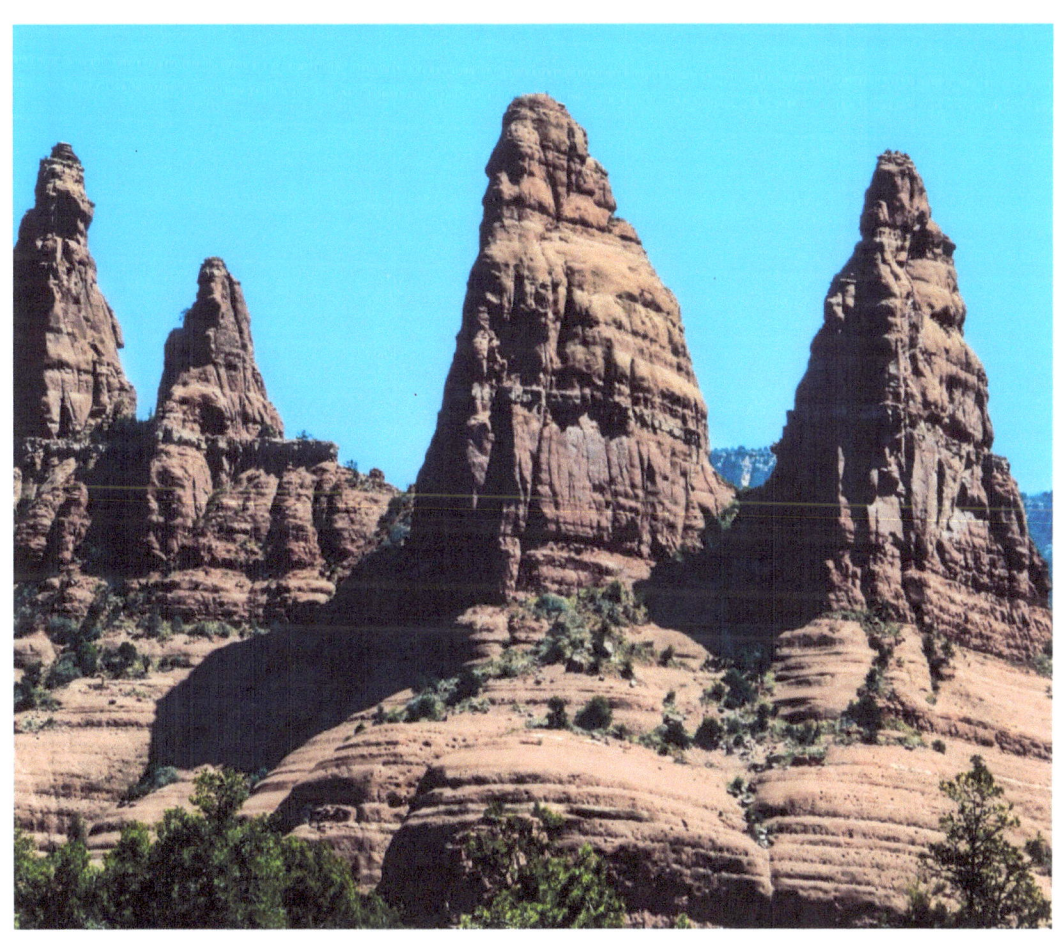

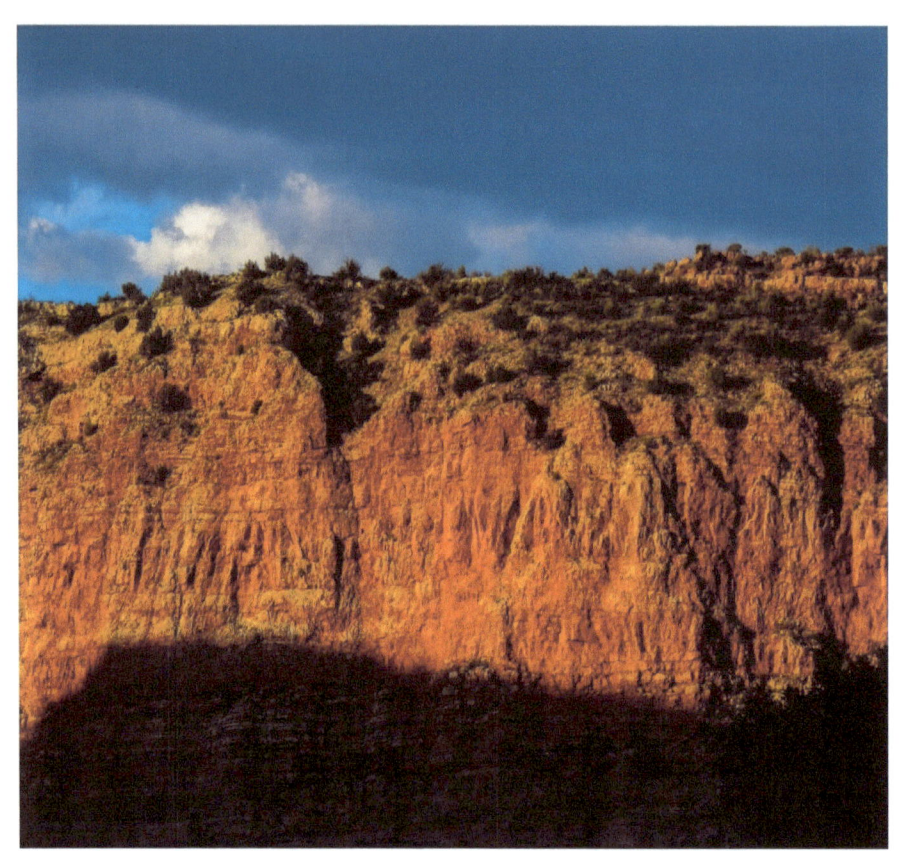

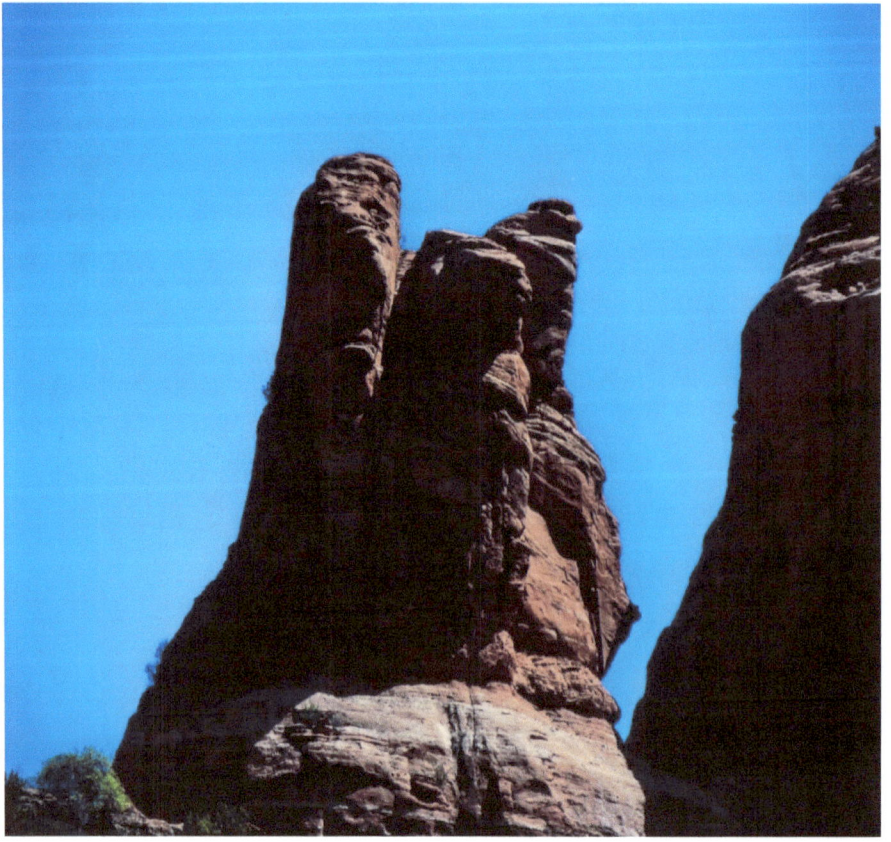

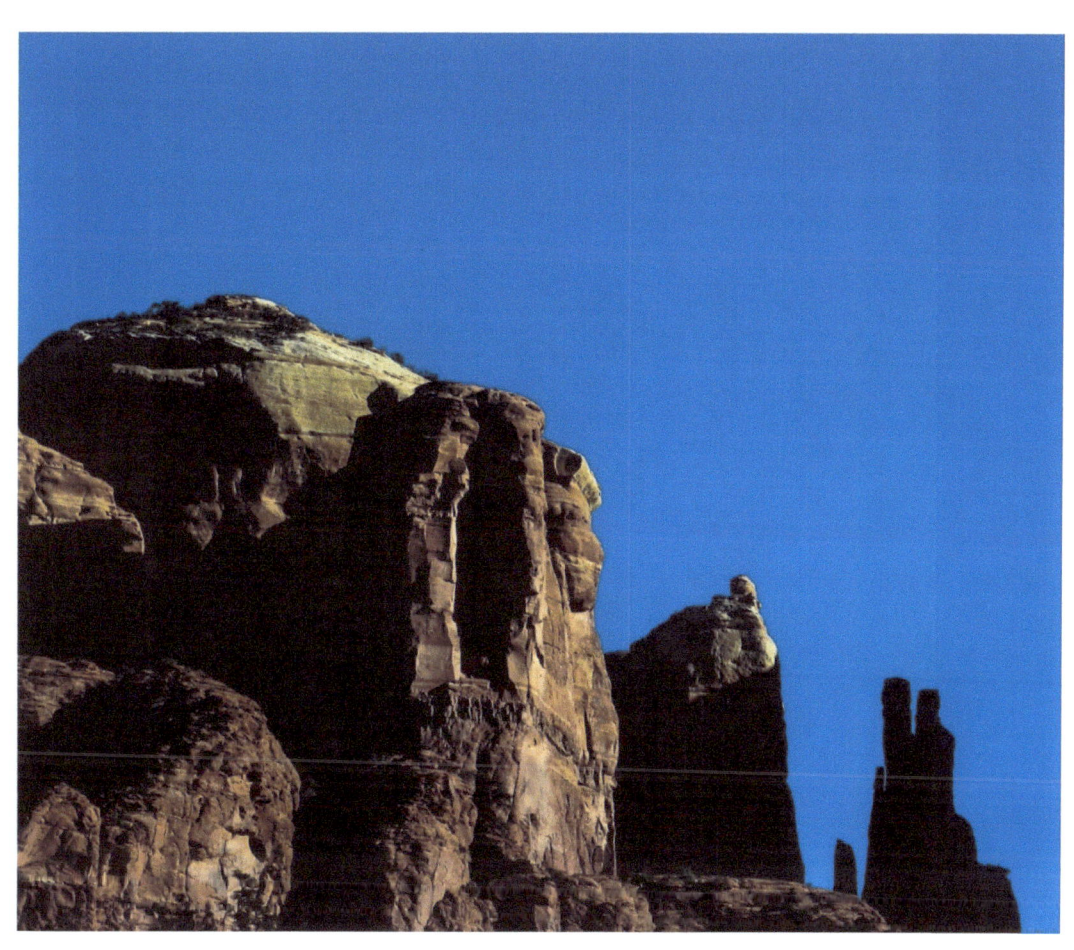

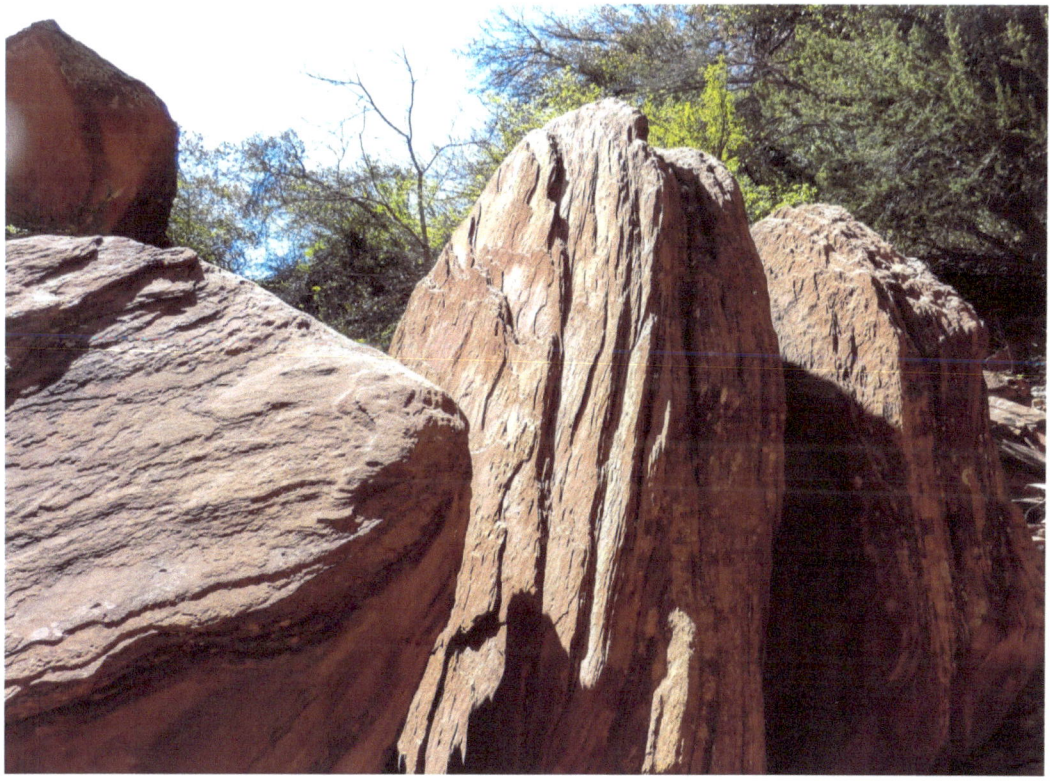

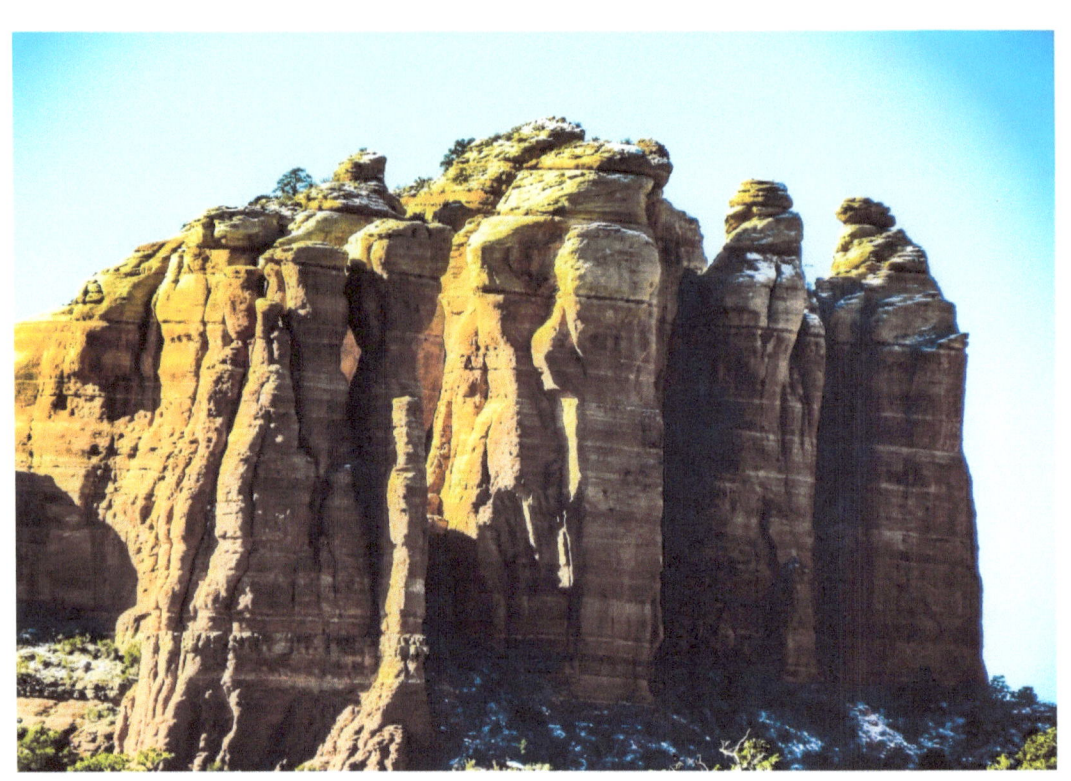

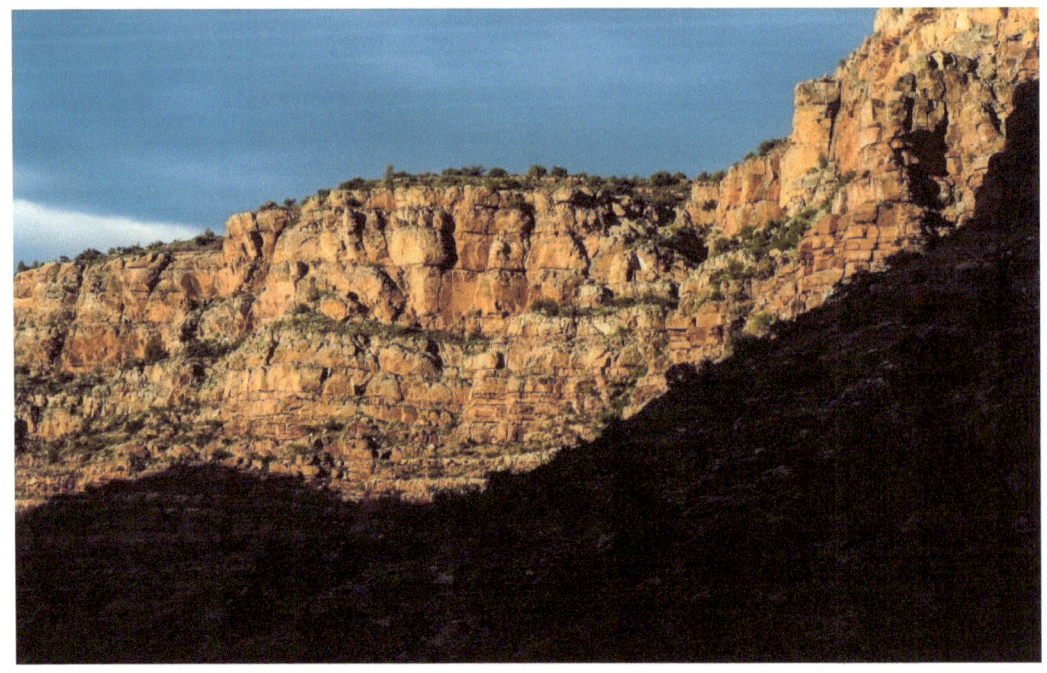

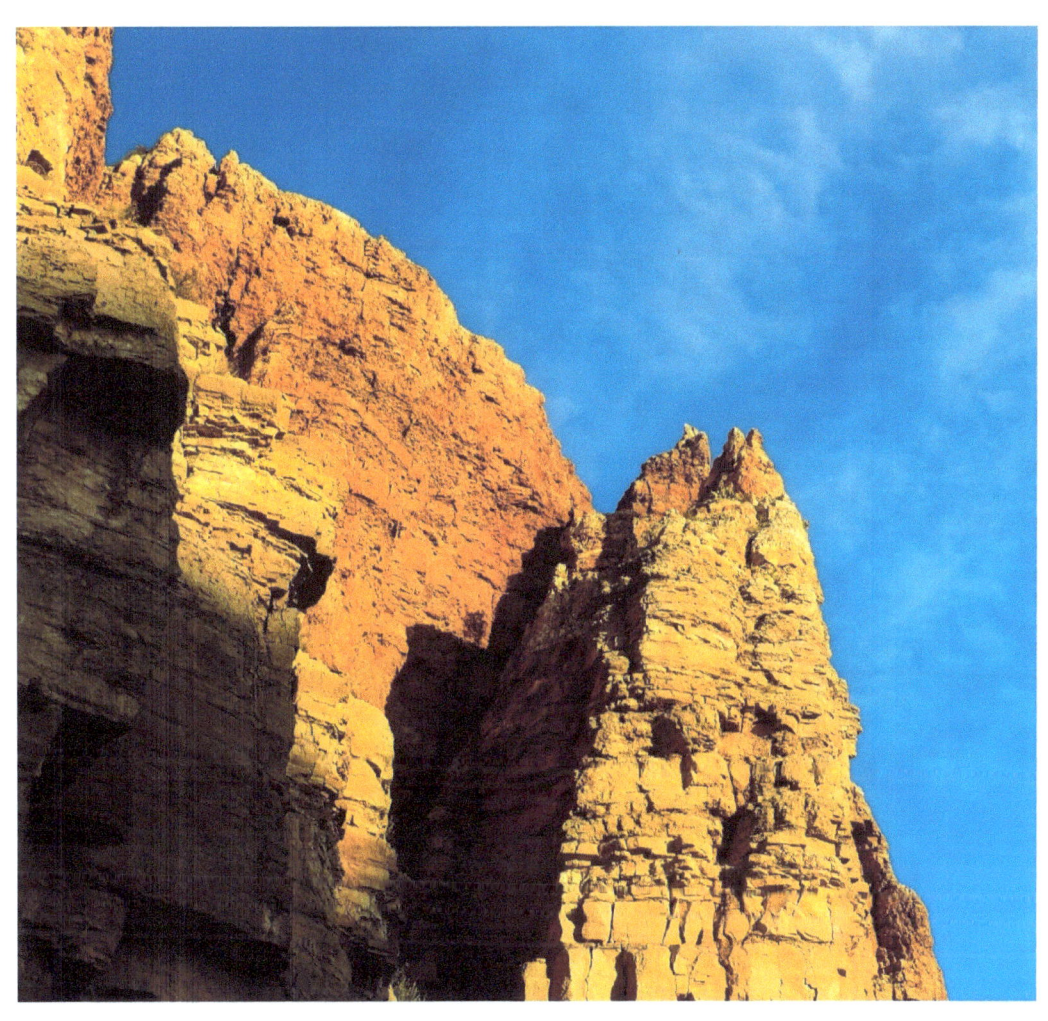

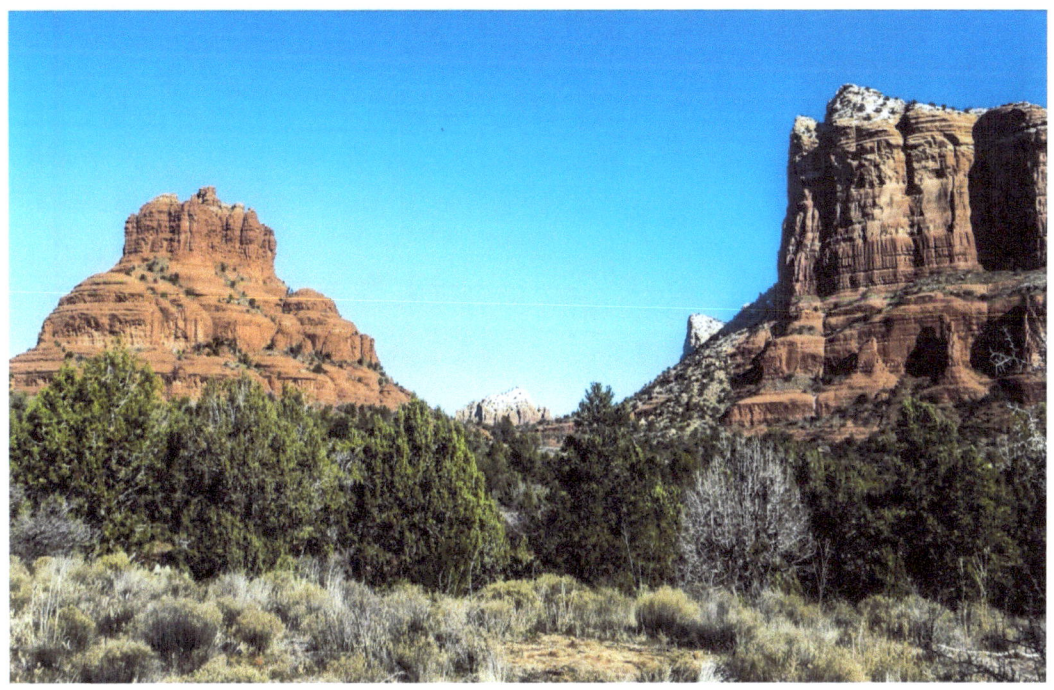

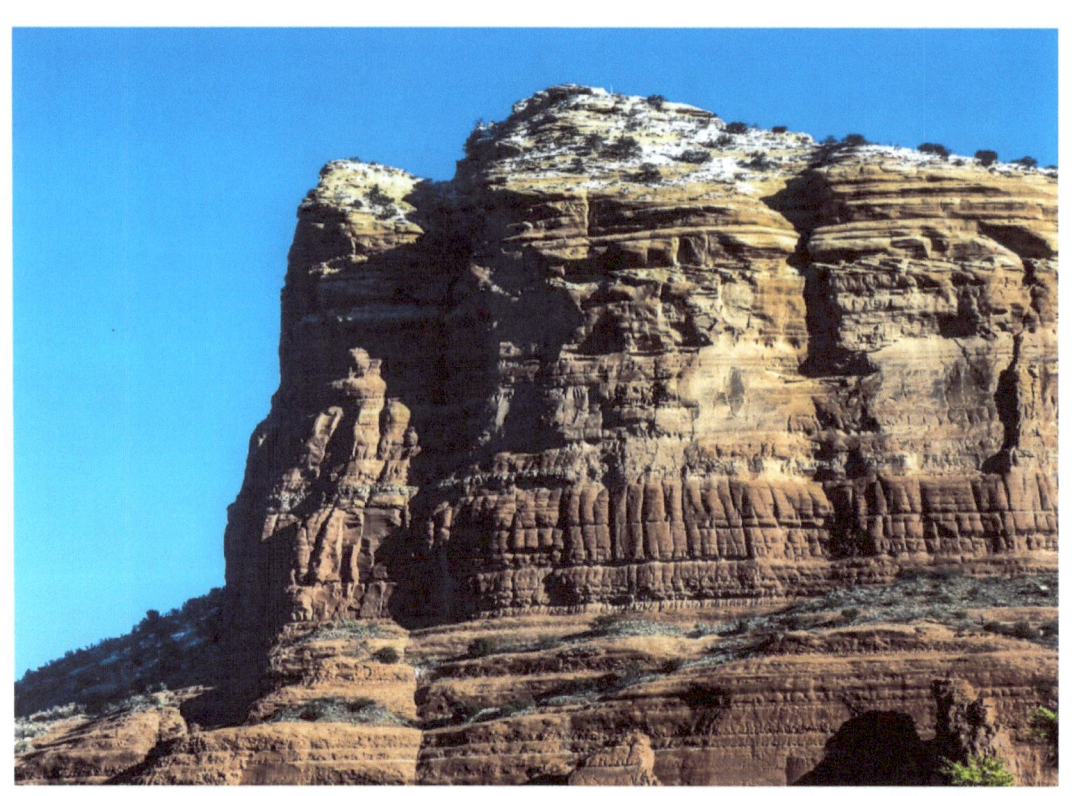

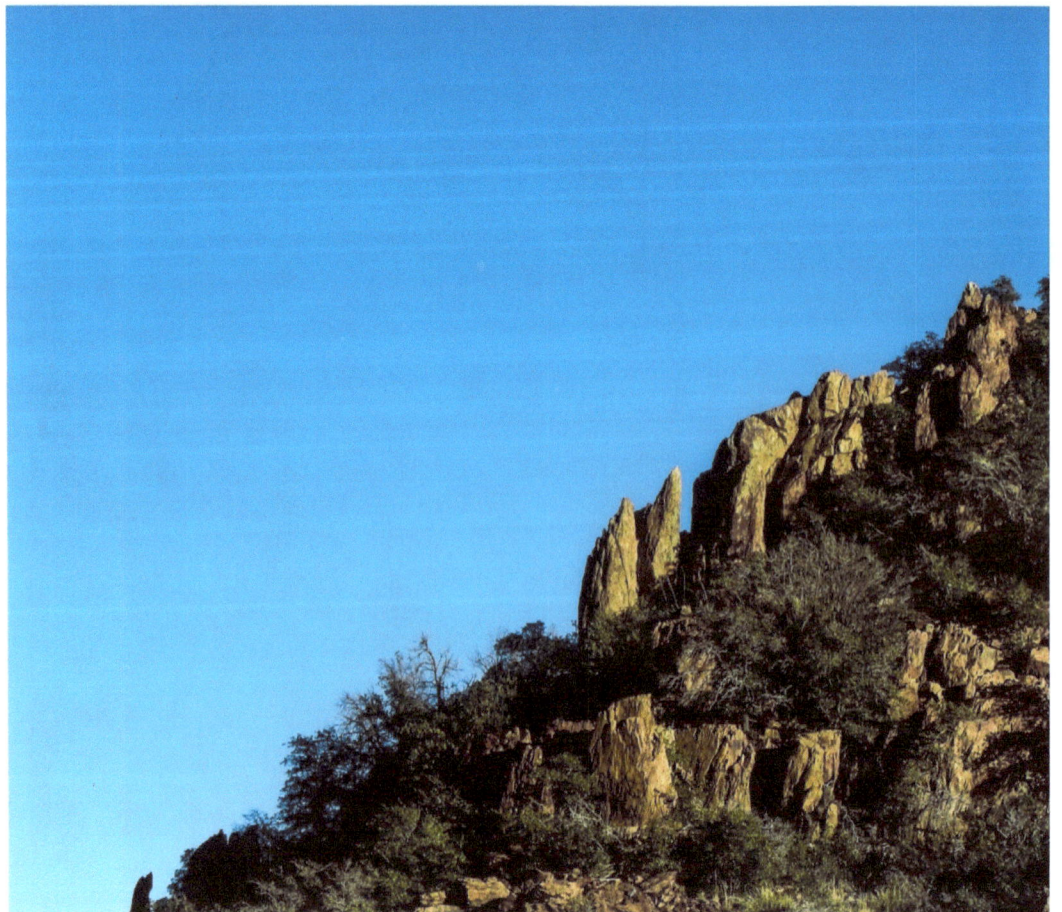

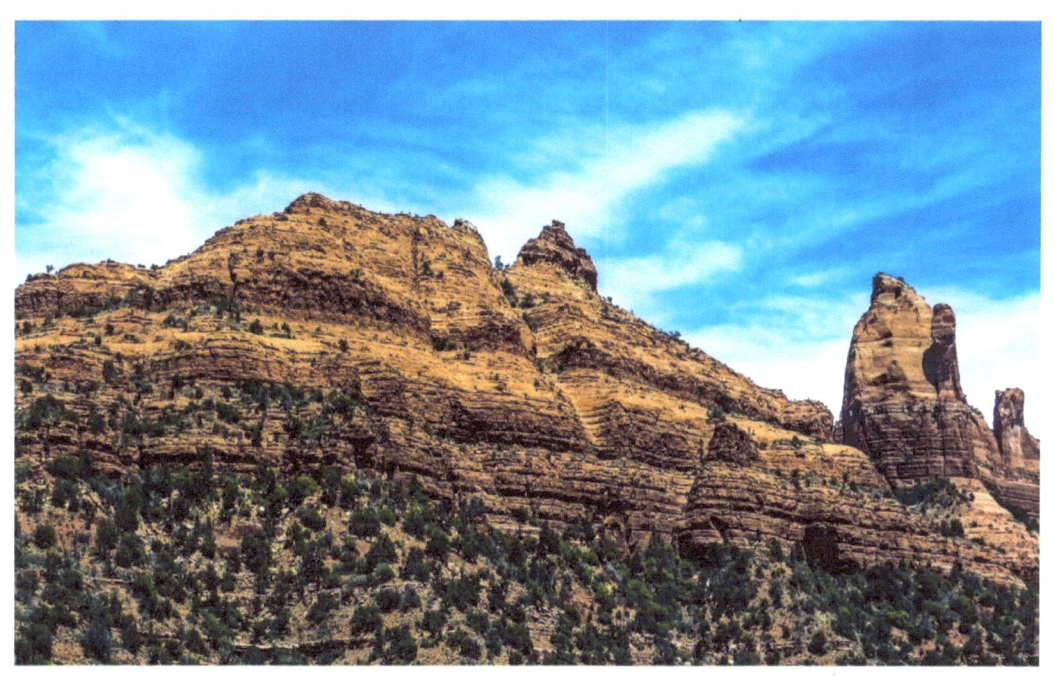

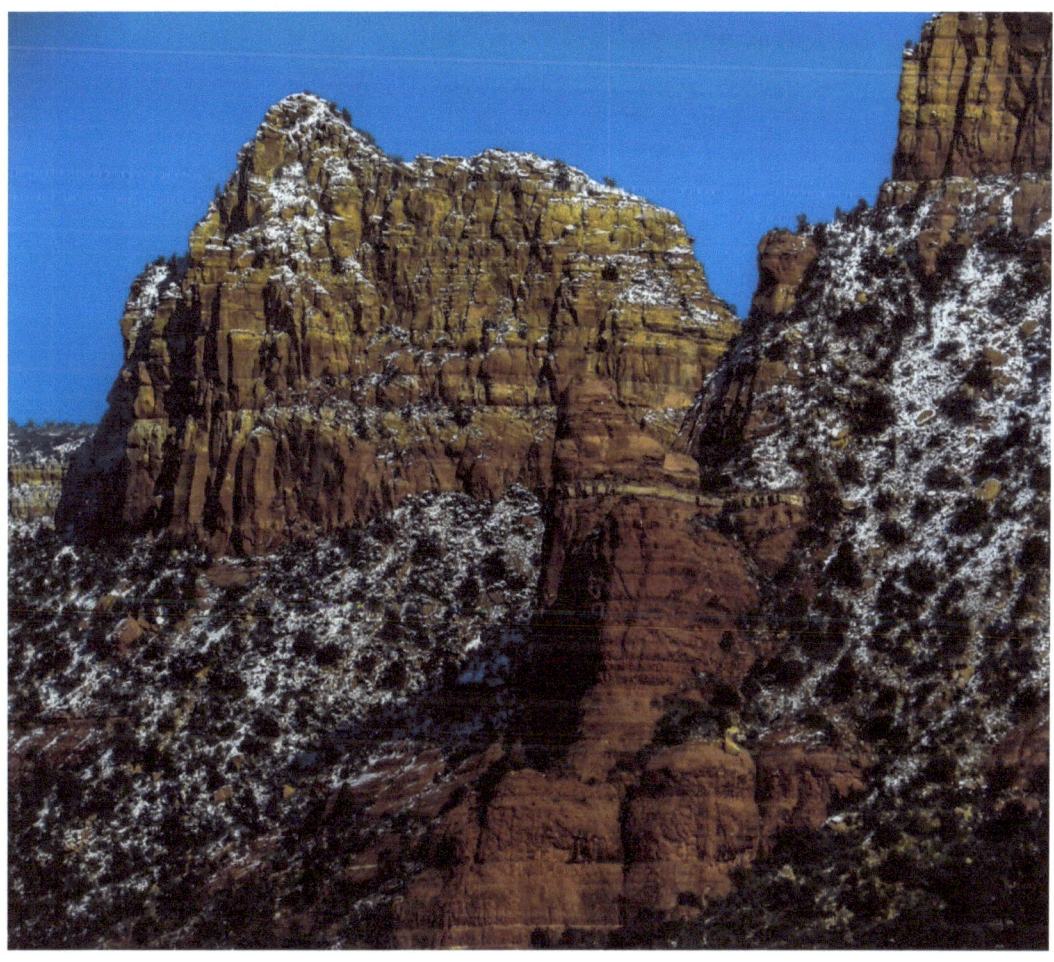

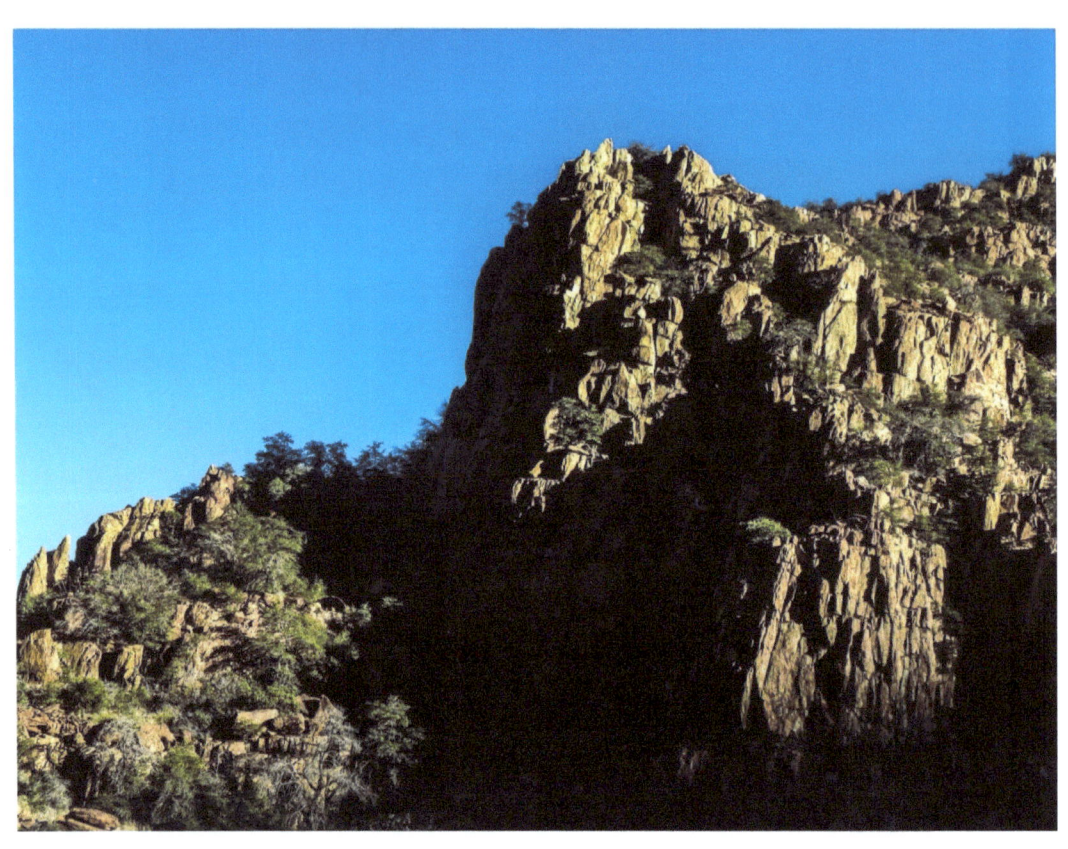

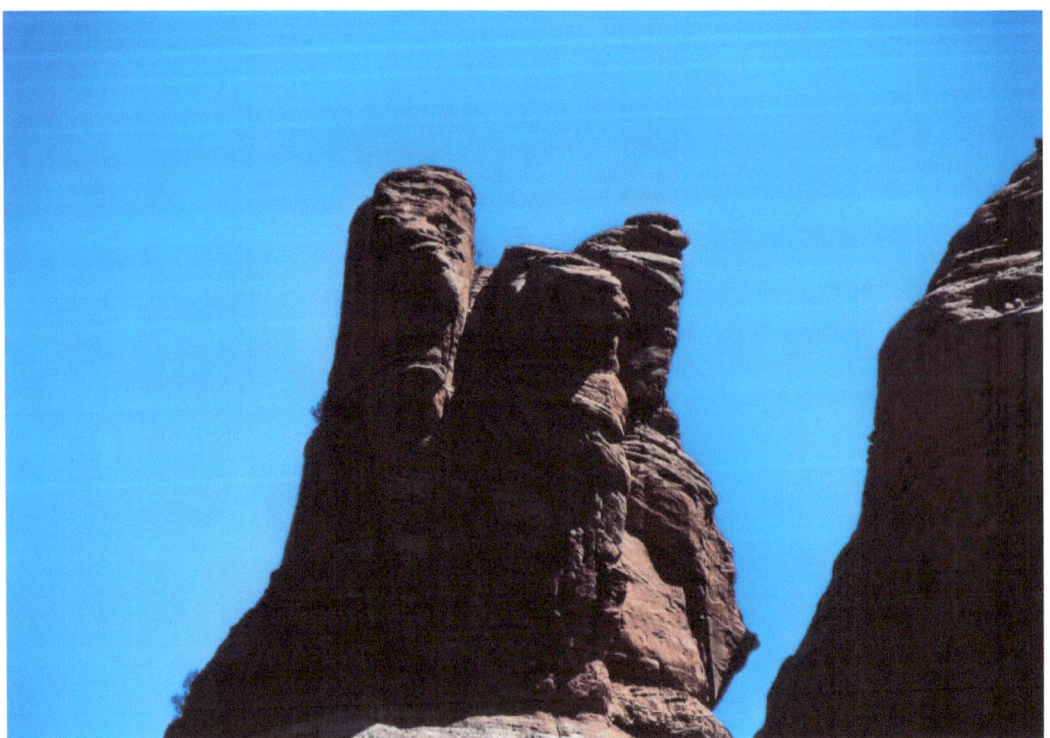

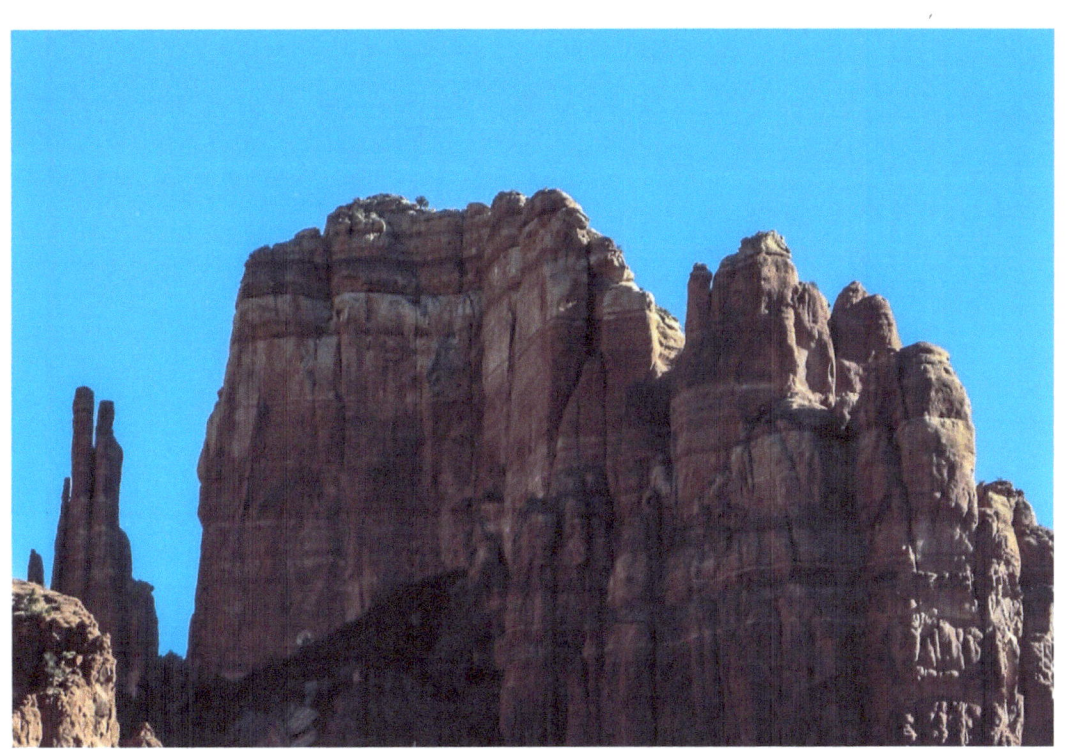

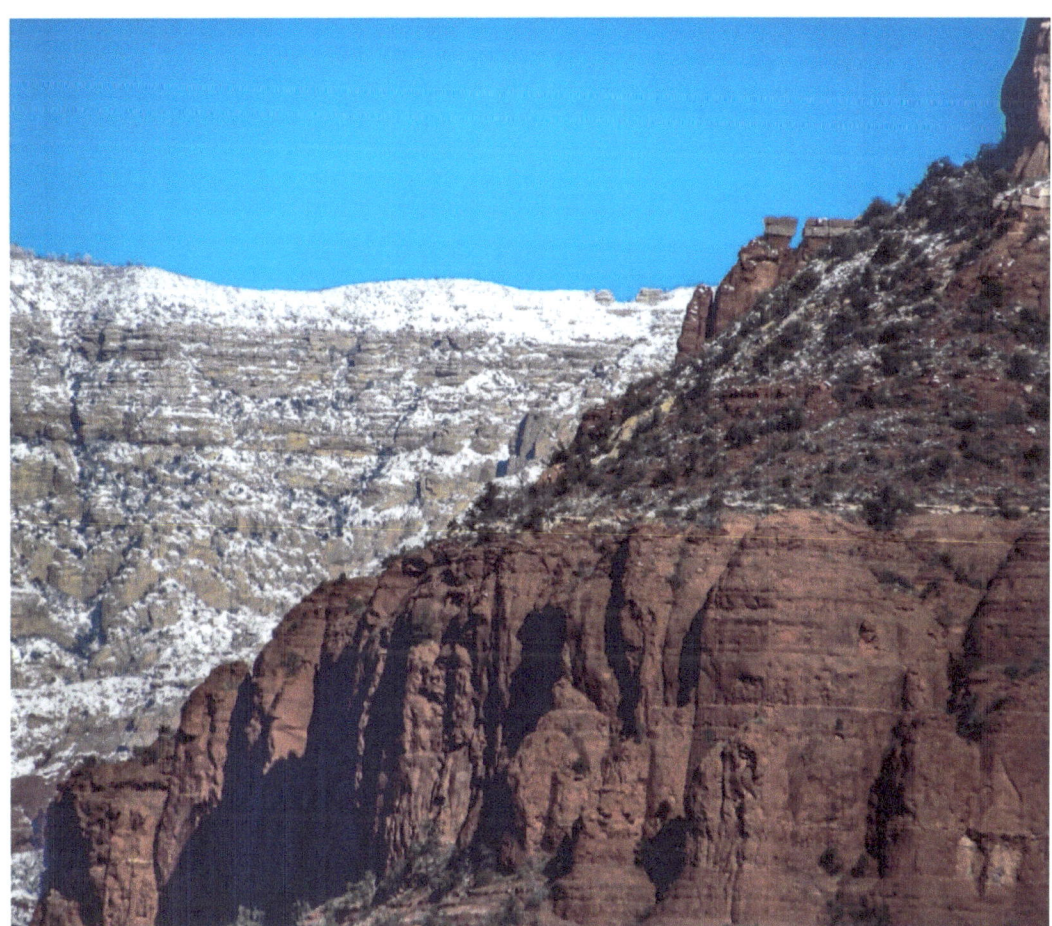

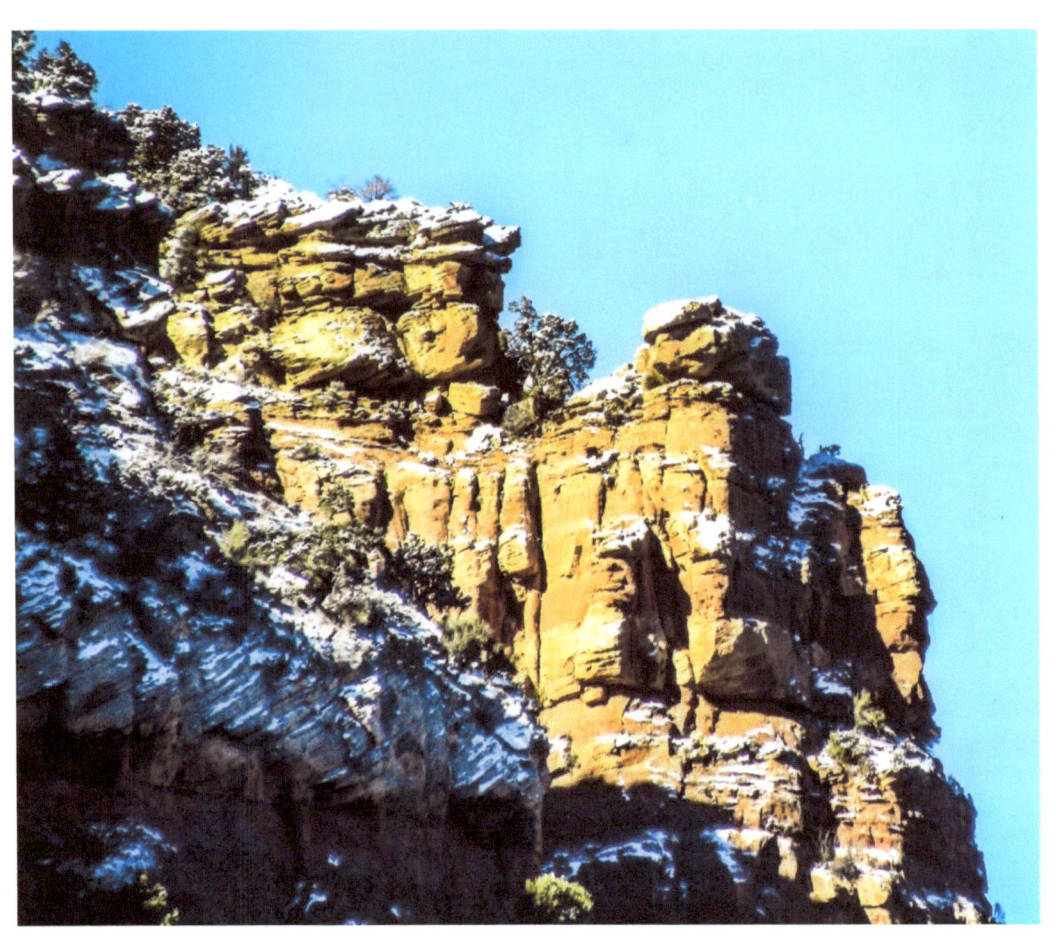

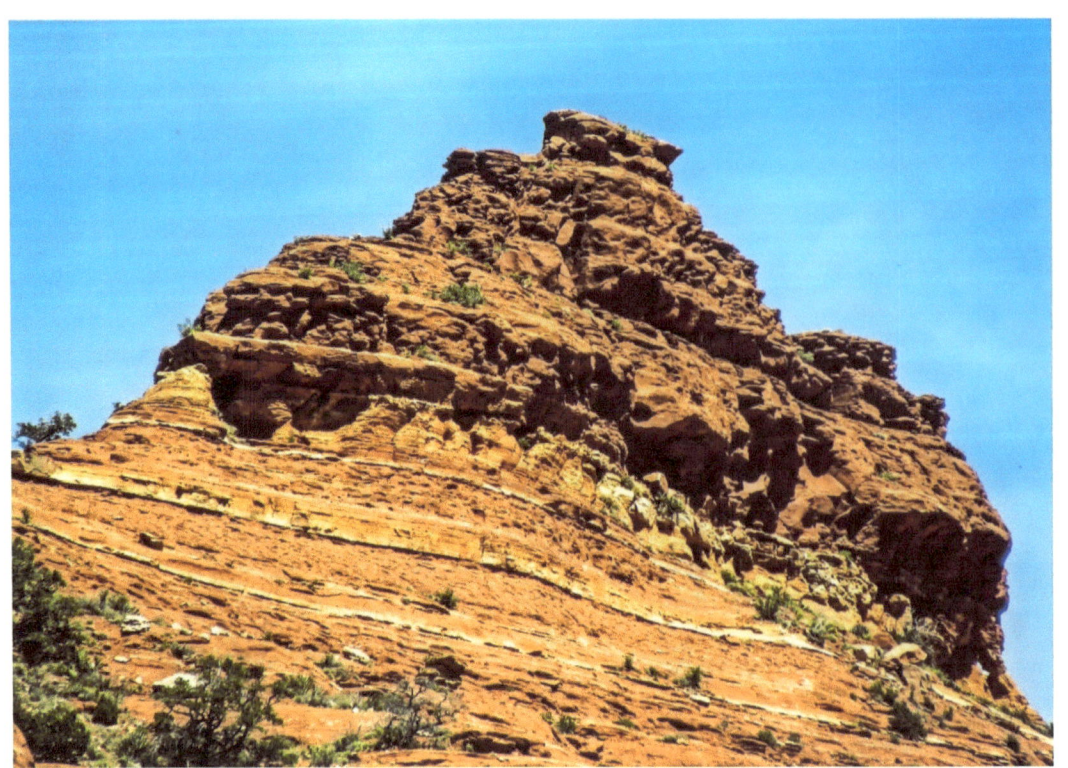

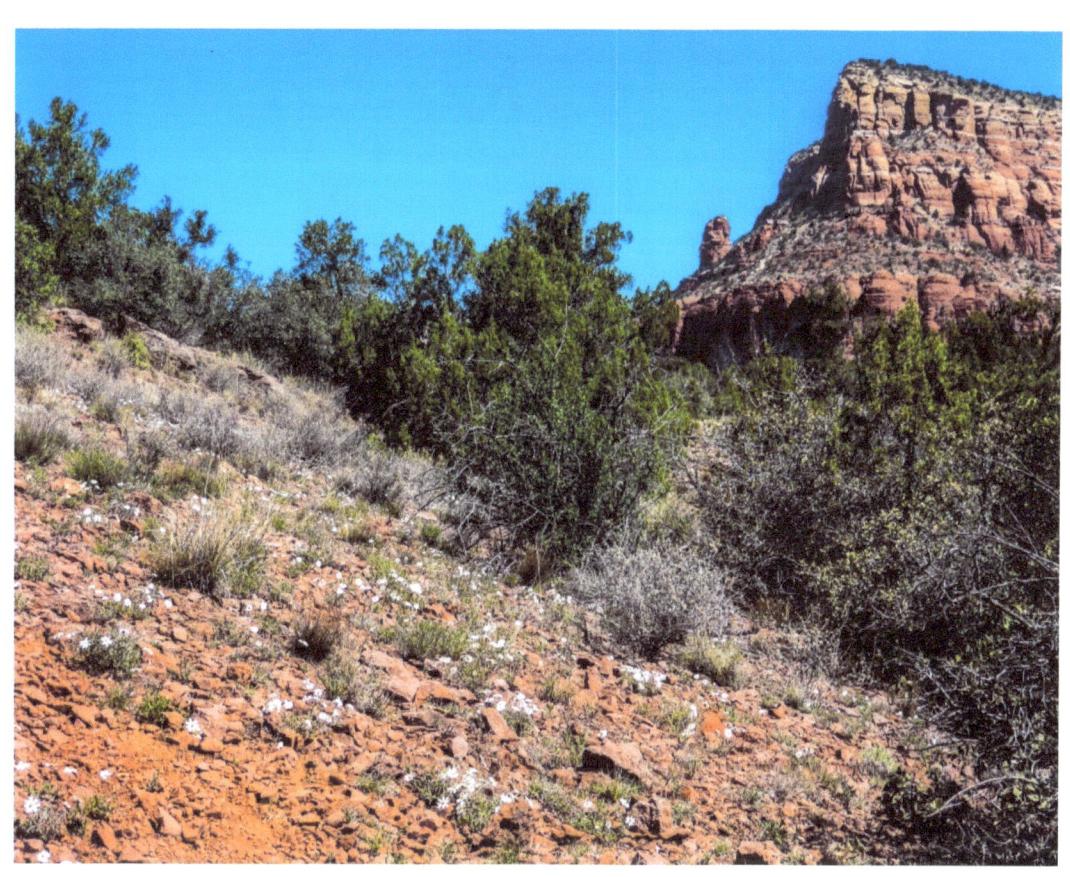

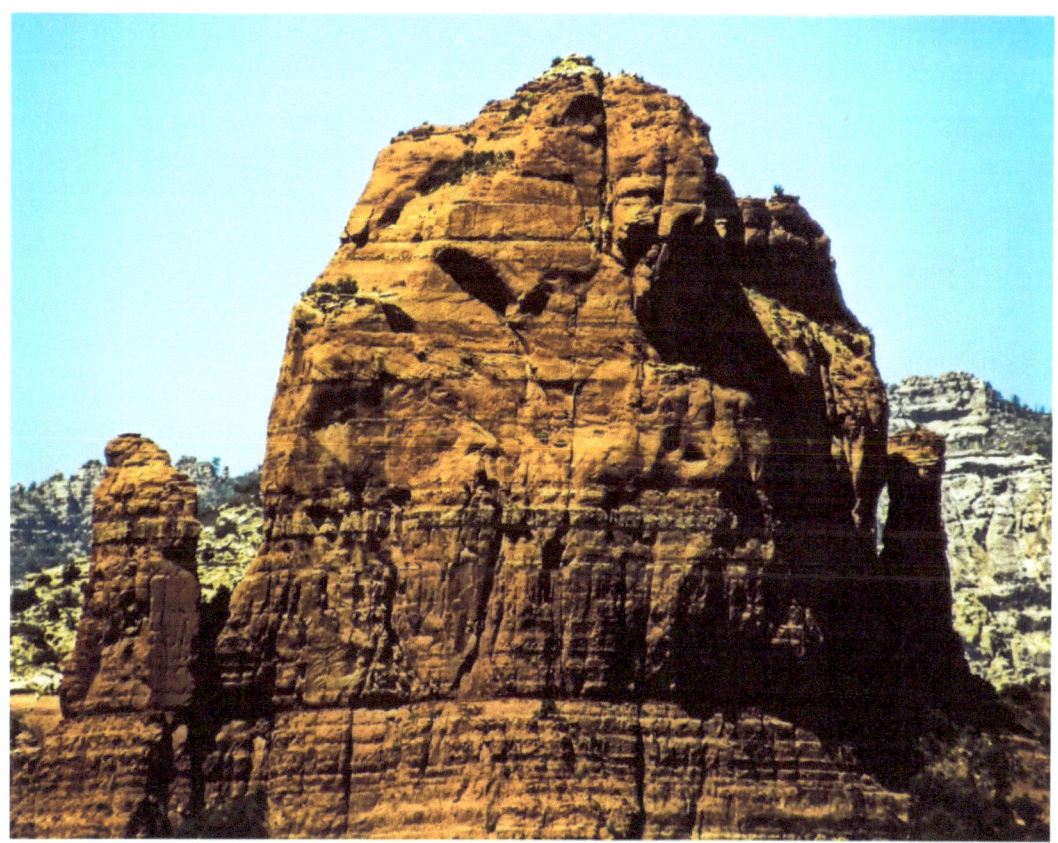

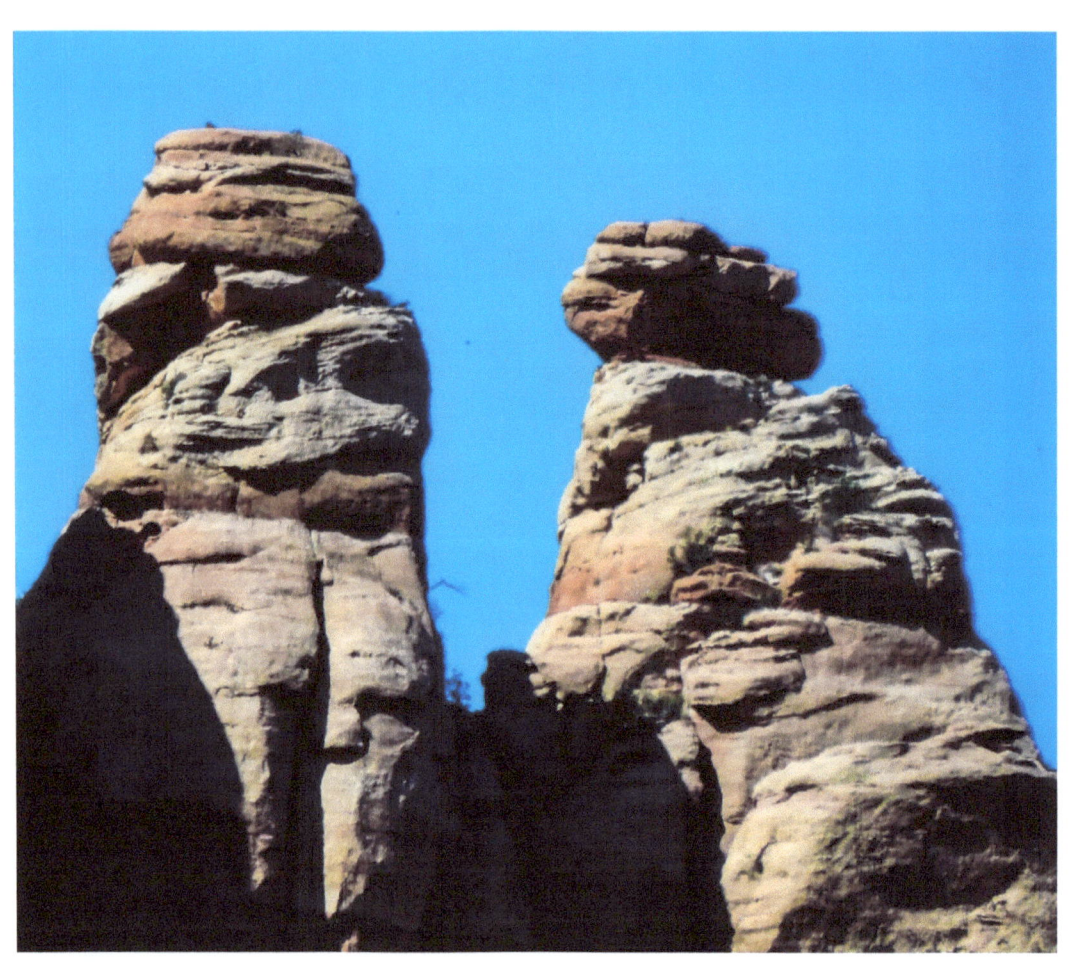

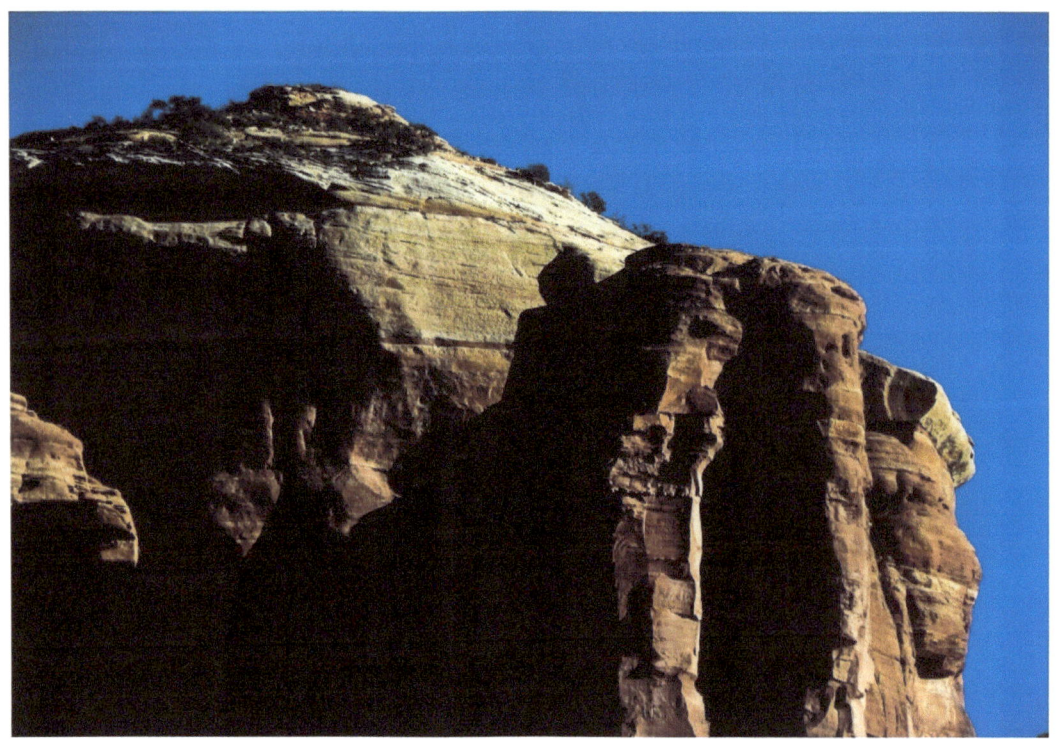

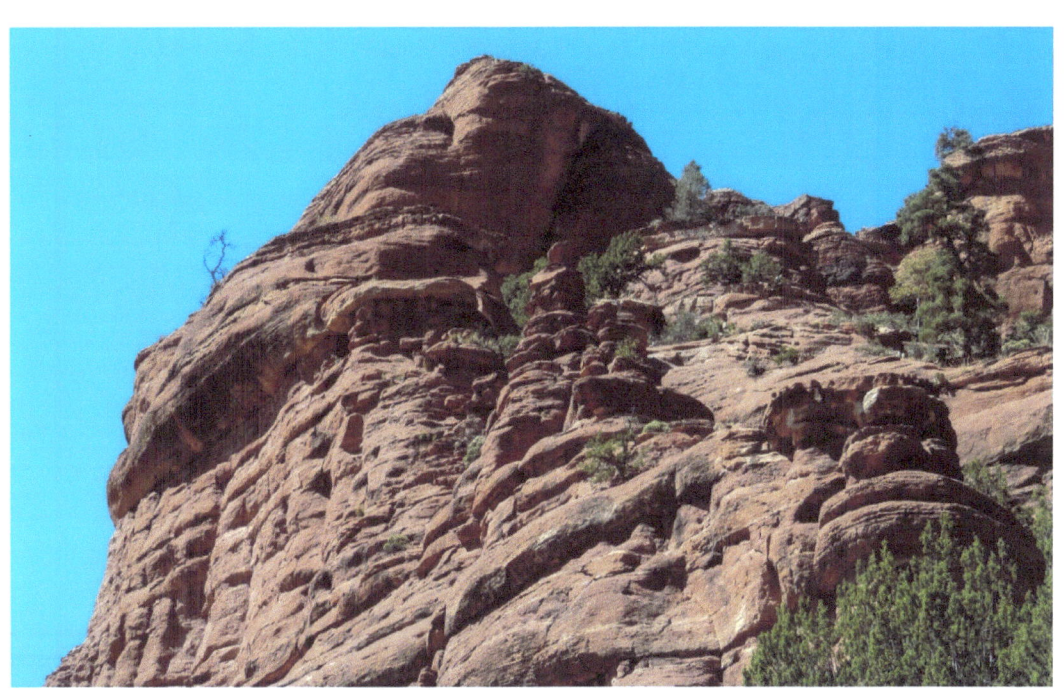

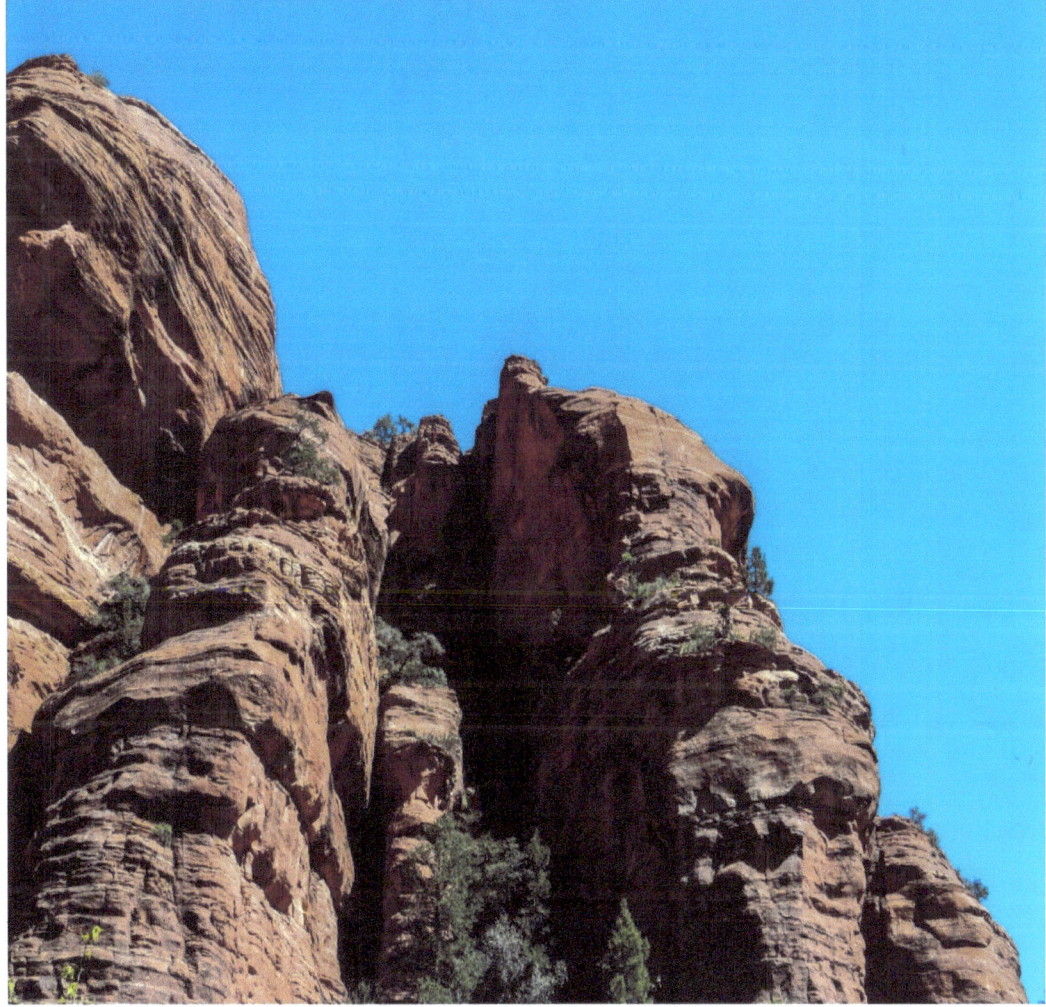

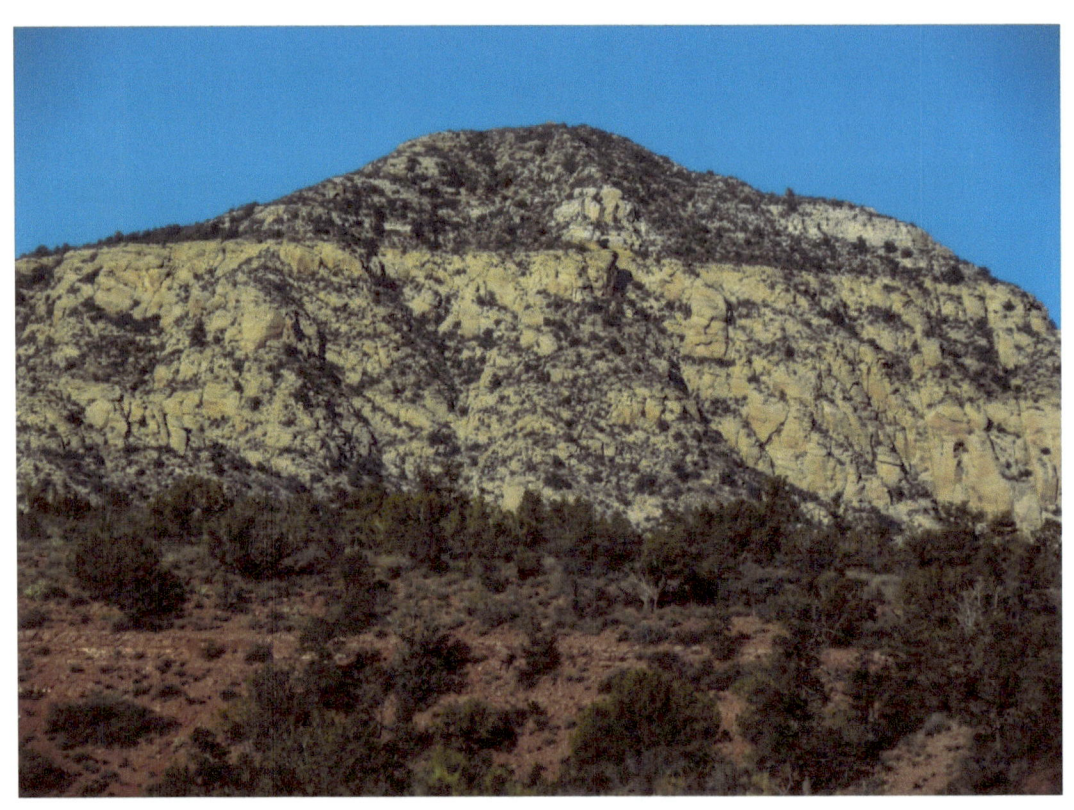

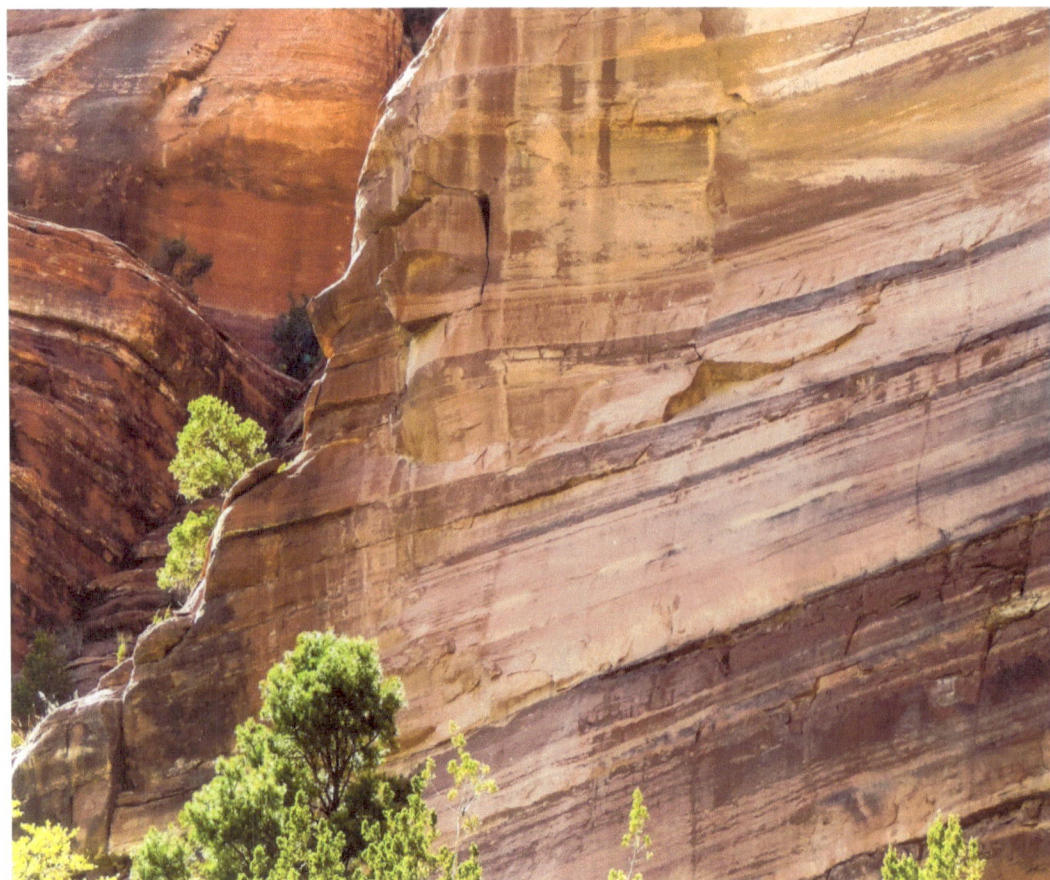